Worked examples in electroheat

by R D Langman

Head of Electricity Utilisation Education,
The Electricity Council
Visiting Professor in Electrical Engineering, Aston University
Director, Electricity Utilisation Studies Unit,
Cambridge University

ASTON/CAMBRIDGE   1987

Contents

Preface

There is a shortage of good teaching material associated with electricity utilisation and excluding motive power. Much of the formative work prepared in the first half of this century in one sector, that of electroheat, now lies buried and forgotten. Indeed, many contemporary academics and students find the topic badly presented, when this dated material is used and whatever is extracted has usually to be re-written using the International System of Units (SI). Taking one particular example, the acclaimed book on Conduction of Heat in Solids by Carslaw and Jaeger[1] hardly commends itself to a modern engineering student and, too often, results from the work are quoted without a practical and theoretical backing. In another area that of field theory and current flow in conductors it is interesting to see how contemporary books use one or two early sources to present the material and avoid quite fundamental questions. For example, how is the skin effect phenomenon described in an internally conducted current in a tube concentric with its return (solid) conductor?

The areas of greatest significance involving power absorption rely on contemporary text-books which treat low power or even communication concepts. Thus in microwave and dielectric heating no book has been written in English for perhaps ten years with the exception of one by Metaxas and Meredith[2] and that is constrained to microwave topics.

The author wished to jog academe into action to respond to what ought to be subject areas of tremendous relevance to the newer industries — what better way than by worked examples? A recent publication by the Union Internationale d'Electrothermie with Professor Kurt Kegel as the Editor[3] gives forty worked examples and certainly this work provided a stimulus and should be used as a parallel source. In this present publication what is attempted is a rather simpler approach. Electroheat is broken down into a series of topics. Each topic is reviewed summarily noting the important and key reference works which are available. A view on the teaching of the topic is given and then selected examples are given. Each example is intended to act as a source of tutorial work in its own right. A good proportion of the examples are of the half an hour examination type.

An attempt has been made not to duplicate other similar ventures. The well-known Schaum series has several potential contenders but for example the excellent outline by Edminister[4] on Electromagnetics makes no mention of heat and how can electromagnetism exist without a parallel thermal effect? Another commendable book by Buckley on Fields[5] is partly redeemable in that the treatment of dielectric loss aspires to a kilowatt or two. Nevertheless one is left with the definitive view that in contemporary society it is possible to take a qualification in electrical and electronic engineering, judged by the courses and new textbooks and not to realise that all of the electricity generated ends up in a thermal form and that approximately half of that is used because of its thermal effects. Indeed in industry forty per cent is applied in non-motive power form and if electricity utilisation is mentioned at all, in syllabii, it would be mainly of concern to drives and their use.

Following an initiative in the mid-seventies by the Electricity Council with the Institution of Electrical Engineers a vigorous attempt to right many wrongs was made with the preparation of a correspondence course on Industrial Process Heating[6]. Reference to this material is made at many points in this work. Few students have 'graduated' from the course and perhaps this is a reflexion on current views on retraining, the intense self-discipline required and the need to acknowledge in contemporary society the passing through such a course with an academic award (to say nothing of other rewards). The course was directed at the postgraduate, post-initial experience phase of the young engineer's career and also at the academic wishing to have an appropriate reference source for relevant courses.

More recently the Electricity Council has published and circulated in its own right limited editions of teaching notes and monographs each devoted to a particular single topic. These have been given a favourable reception. Nevertheless it is with the conventional routes in academe and industry that good text books should occur and such a pump priming activity may hopefully be the catalyst.

Acknowledgement to the help received from the author's colleagues Dr A C Metaxas and Dr A M Featherstone is made. With the author they are attempting to develop the material in the UK at Cambridge and Aston Universities respectively. Again the work at Loughborough University over the last decade has given much source material and the help of Mr H Barber, Dr J E Harry and Dr L Hobson has been quite fundamental. Outside these three universities of Aston, Cambridge and Loughborough other friends in UK academe have been canvassed for help and when usable

material has been forthcoming its source is acknowledged.
Particular mention is made of the members of the Education and
Training Committee of the British National Committee of
Electroheat and especially Dr P. Tsappi of the North East London
Polytechnic. In its own right this committee and its controlling
body, the British National Committee of Electroheat, has been
responsible for publishing material of direct educational value. One
such source is a list of electroheat references[7]. The present work
however does list an independent bibliography which the author
has found personally of value.

What does the author hope from this work? First of all the
realisation that electrical engineering and particularly power
engineering must not be allowed to continue as a Cinderella area.
There is a need for the development of utilisation skills — after all
for every power engineer on the 'supply' side there must be at least
a tenfold demand on the 'customer' side. Secondly here are a
number of topics fundamental to the wealth creation needs of
manufacturing and processing industries just waiting for proper
academic treatment. That there is a need is readily emphasised by
examining the bibliographies which all too often have to refer to
works out of print and are almost forgotten. This is a subject area
which is practised but not taught. Thirdly there remains much
work undertaken outside academe which has yet to find its way
into syllabii and mention by way of example must be made of the
output of the first two decades of operation at the Electricity
Council's Research Centre at Capenhurst near Chester, much of
which is devoted to this area of work[8]. Finally, if the interest can
be generated the publication of a second book of worked examples
in ten years time will be found unnecessary since there will be a
good foundation of fundamental and specialised books for students
and scholars making such a work irrelevant.

Each working chapter follows a common format. A discussion on the
topic reviews how the author sees it in an educational environment.
The final section of each chapter lists the worked examples.

Naturally the author has been through each example and hopefully
errors should be small. It is too much however to expect that a first
edition will be error free. The author would welcome any errors
being brought to his attention.

The following notation has been used

E	generic phasor
$\hat{E}$	peak value
$\bar{E}$	phasor (independent of time)
$\hat{E}^*; E^*$	conjugates

R.D.L.
Cambridge 1987

List of Symbols

Each symbol is defined either in the set question or in the associated solution. Thus there may be some inconsistencies occurring as between the various sources used. Nevertheless the symbols and abbreviations will in general conform to international standards, although non-standard quantities will frequently arise due to the specialised nature of the topics. Again, except where common usage of a specialised nature exists SI units are used. All quantities with subscripts are defined in the text. Standard constants are (usually) stated in each example quoted.

Symbol	Term	Unit-symbol
A	current	A
A	area	m^2
a	distance	m
a	constant	—
b	constant	—
b	distance	m
B	magnetic flux density	T, Wbm^{-2}
c	constant	—
c	velocity of light	$m\,s^{-1}$
C	specific density	$kg.m^{-3}$
C	numeric ratio	—
C	specific heat capacity	$Jm^{-1}\,K^{-1}$
C	capacitance	F
C	electron charge	As
D_p	penetration depth	m
D, d	diameter	m
E	electric field strength	Vm^{-1}
E	power density	$W\,m^{-2}$
E	radiative flux	W
$\dot{e}$	electron charge	—
f	frequency	s^{-1}
F	force	N
H	(holding) power	W
H	heat content	kWh/t
H	magnetic field intensity	Am^{-1}, Atm^{-1}
h	Planck's constant	Js
h	height	m
h	thickness	m
I	current	A
J	current density	A/m^2
j	square root of minus one	—
k	power loss	$W\,K^{-1}$
k	thermal conductivity	$Wm^{-1}\,K^{-1}$ (or $JK^{-1}\,m^{-1}$)

Symbol	Term	Unit-symbol
K, k	numeric ratio constant	—
K	Boltzmann constant	JK^{-1} (1.38×10^{-23})
L, l	inductance	H
L	length	m
m	electron mass	kg
M	moisture content (relative)	—
m ,	mass	kg
N	number of terms	—
n	index	—
n	population of electrons	—
p	power density	$W\,m^{-2}$
p	pressure gradient	—
P	active power	W
Q, q	heat flow	W or J
Q	Q-factor	—
r	radius	m
R	radius	m
R	resistance	Ω
S	specific heat	$Jm^{-1}\,K^{-1}$
S	stirring force density	N/m^{-2}
T	temperature	K
T	tonnage rate	$t\,s^{-1}$
t	time	s
u	velocity	ms^{-1}
v, V	voltage	V
w	length	m
Z	impedance	Ω
Z	distance	m
V	voltage	V
X, x	distance	m
x	reactance	Ω
Y, y	distance	m
Z	length	m
Z, z	impedance	Ω
α^2	diffusivity	$m^2\,s^{-1}$
α	absorption coefficient	—
Γ, γ	numeric ratio	—
γ	density	$kg\,m^{-3}$
δ	skin depth	m
Δ, δ	small increment	—
ε	absolute permittivity	F/m
ε_0	free space permittivity	F/m
ε_r	relative permittivity	F/m
ε	error	—

Symbol	Term	Unit-symbol
ε	emissivity	—
ζ	efficiency	—
θ	temperature	K
θ	degrees	—
λ	wavelength	m
μ	absolute permeability	Hm^{-1}
μ_0	free space permeability	Hm^{-1}
μ_r	relative permeability	Hm^{-1}
v	voltage	V
ρ	resistivity	Ωm
ρ	density	$kg\,m^3$
σ	conductivity	Sm^{-1}
σ	Stefan-Boltzmann constant	$J/(m^2sK)$ $[5.67 \times 10^{-8}]$
ω	angular velocity	$radians.s^{-1}$
τ	time ratio	—
τ	time constant	s
τ	stress	N
ϕ	angle	radian
χ	polarisation	—

Introduction

Our subject is electroheat with an emphasis on heating within industrial processes. Where is electricity used, where is it generated, what fuels are used, how much does it cost ... all these are questions which the enquiring student will want answered preferably early on in a course. Nothing dates a written work more than examples on economics (the taunt used to be 'economic questions remain unaltered only the answers change').

Fortunately there is a convenient remedy. Annually the Electricity Council publish a Handbook of Statistics[9] and in this little gem will be found most of the answers to these starting questions. From it one can find how much electricity is sold, to whom and what the revenues were. Breakdowns of sales to industrial sectors can be found so that we can find for example that the iron and steel industry accounts for roughly 10% of the electricity sold to industry in England and Wales and in turn this represents about 4% of the total electricity generated.

What is not so conveniently available is the distribution among the technological uses of electricity. For this information one has to search for national energy audits. The last detailed audit was made in the sixties.

An interesting source by G Leach and others[10] suggests how the UK could improve its energy usage efficiency and uses an updated extrapolated version of the audit. Of interest is the submission to the Sizewell enquiries by the CEGB in which various scenarios of usage patterns are suggested for the year 2000[11].

In broad terms an examination of these data shows that about 60% of all electricity in industry is used initially for some form of motive power. This application sector is likely to decline. In industry process heating represents 10% of the total electricity sold to industry and in absolute terms is increasing.

These process heating applications may first be considered in broad terms[12]. The tremendous range of power from a few watts for perhaps a laser to a hundred mega-watts or so for an arc furnace indicates the scope of the topic (Figure I1). Running in parallel are the physical mechanisms which will be encountered (Figure I2) and their associated power densities (Figure I3). Classification of

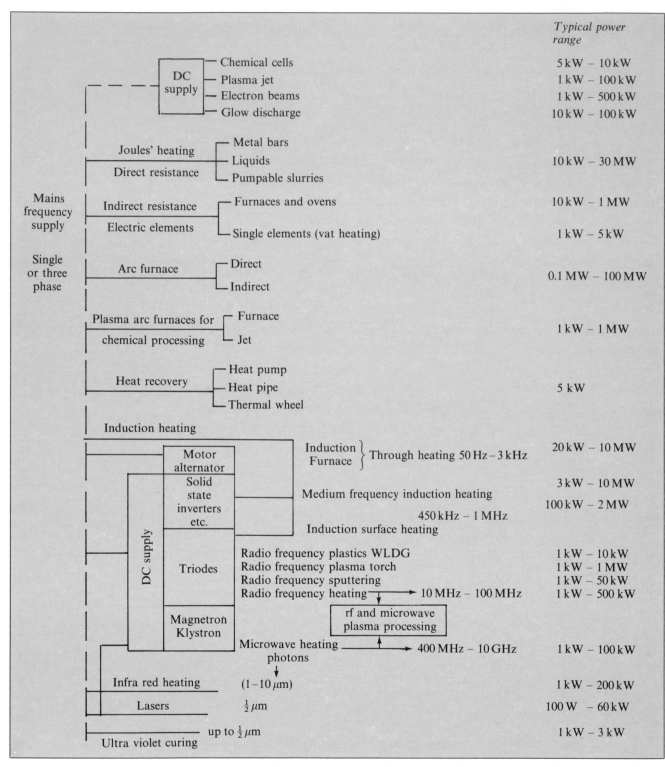

Figure I1 *Classification of electrical utilisation processes*

process and application is difficult. In the current work it is chosen to examine the topics sequentially in a rough but logical and self evident order.

Finally many engineering courses reflect the requirement for the future engineer to know something about the economics of the

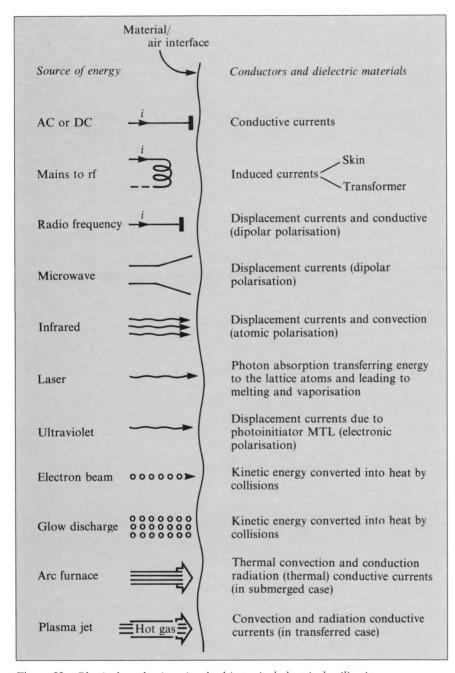

Figure I2 *Physical mechanisms involved in typical electrical utilisation processes*

systems and their components. In this case inevitably one is drawn into the area of tariffs. In the UK each electricity area board is responsible for publishing its own tariffs which in turn reflect the cost of generation (in England and Wales the CEGB publish a Supply Tariff which in turn is reflected in the area board's tariffs[9]). A convenient review of UK tariffs is given in the Electricity Supply Handbook[13]. No further attention to this subject is given in this work. However, the decision making mechanisms behind the choice of a maximum demand level can be quite torturous and an example involving a large load (arc furnaces) and the control of energy to a

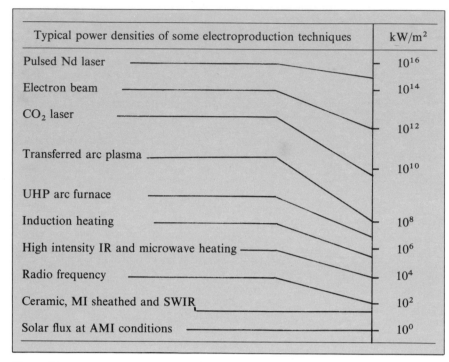

Typical power densities of some electroproduction techniques	kW/m²

Pulsed Nd laser — 10^{16}

Electron beam — 10^{14}

CO₂ laser — 10^{12}

Transferred arc plasma — 10^{10}

UHP arc furnace —

Induction heating — 10^{8}

High intensity IR and microwave heating — 10^{6}

Radio frequency — 10^{4}

Ceramic, MI sheathed and SWIR — 10^{2}

Solar flux at AMI conditions — 10^{0}

Figure I3

fixed MD is given in Chapter 7. A simple problem comparing two competing electrical loads working to a common tariff is given in the first example I1.

I1

An industrial consumer has an existing balanced 3-phase load of 1.5 MVA at p.f. 0.9 lagging. A proposed new heating load can be achieved by either direct resistance heating or induction. The table gives relevant information for the two alternatives.

Repayment of capital must be at the rate of 20% per annum for each scheme. The consumer's tariff is: £3 per KVA (30-min average) per month, and 4p per kWh. If the existing load and the new load are to be operated simultaneously for 12 hours per day and 20 days per month, determine which of the two new proposals will be more economic.

How may maximum demand be reduced?

	Direct Resistance Heating	Induction Heating
Capital cost	£0.8 m	£1 m
Load (balanced)	1 MVA on for 10 min, off for 5 min.	2 MVA on for 12 min, off for 3 min.
Power factor	unity	0.3 lagging

What additional factors would be considered to make a choice between these plants?

(Courtesy of Aston University B.Eng. Finals 1985 — modified by the author)

Solution

	Direct Resistance Scheme	Induction Heating Scheme
Capital charges per month	$\frac{0.2}{12} \times £0.8\,\text{m} = £13{,}333$	$\frac{0.2}{12} \times £1\,\text{m} = £16{,}667$
Existing load: P_e Q_e S_e	$1500.0.9 = 1.35\,\text{MW}$ $1500 \times 0.4359 = 0.654\,\text{MVAR}$ $1500\,\text{kW}\ 1.5\,\text{MVA}$	$1.35\,\text{MW}$ $0.654\,\text{MVAR}$ $1500\,\text{kW}\ 1.5\,\text{MVA}$

Capital charges per month	$\frac{0.2}{12} \times £0.8\,\text{m} = £13{,}333$	$\frac{0.2}{12} \times £1\,\text{m} = £16{,}667$
New load: P_n Q_n S_n	$1\,\text{MW}$ $0\,\text{MVAR}$ $1\,\text{MVA}$	$2.03 = 0.6\,\text{MW}$ $2 \times 0.954 = 1.91\,\text{MVAR}$ $2\,\text{MVA}$
Total combined P_T new + old load: Q_T $\sqrt{P_T + Q_T} =$ S_T S_{av}* M.D. Charge £3 per kVA kWh per hr kWh cost per day at 4p for 12 hr per month	$1.35 + 1 = 2.35\,\text{MW}$ $0.654 + 0 = 0.654\,\text{MVAR}$ $\sqrt{2.35^2 + 0.654^2} = 2.44\,\text{MVA}$ $(2.44 \times \frac{2}{3} + 1.5 \times \frac{1}{3}) = 2.13\,\text{MVA}$ $£3 \times 2.13.10^3 = £6{,}390$ $2.35 \times 10^3 \times \frac{2}{3} + 1.35 \times 10^3 \times \frac{1}{3}$ $= 2020\,\text{kWh}$ $\frac{2020}{100} \times 12.4 = £970$ $20 \times £970 = £19{,}400$	$1.35 + 0.6 = 1.95\,\text{MW}$ $0.654 + 1.91 = 2.564\,\text{MVAR}$ $\sqrt{1.95^2 + 2.564^2} = 3.22\,\text{MVA}$ $(3.22 \times \frac{4}{5} + 1.5 \times \frac{1}{6}) = 2.876\,\text{MVA}$ $£3 \times 2.88.10^3 = £8{,}640$ $1.95 \times 10^3 \times \frac{4}{5} + 1.35 \times 10^3 \times \frac{1}{5}$ $= 1830\,\text{kWh}$ $\frac{1830}{100} \times 12.4 = £878$ $20 \times £878 = £17{,}560$
Total cost per month	$13{,}333 + 6{,}390 + 19{,}400$ $= £39{,}123$	$16{,}667 + 8{,}640 + 17{,}560$ $= £42{,}867$

*This assumes that optimum synchronism occurs and the cycles are continuous.

ie Direct Resistance Heating is marginally cheaper

Maximum demand may be reduced by installing power factor correction at additional capital cost in the case of the induction equipment. However, some savings in 'copper' would arise.

Maximum demand may be reduced in both cases by load shedding during peak periods within a lower MD target than 2.35 MW and 1.95 MW respectively.

Some of the additional factors which would be considered in choosing between the two systems include:

i)   Instrumentation and control systems.
ii)   Induction heating is non-contact.
iii)   Direct resistance heating being contact fed will have 'cold' ends which will require 'stand-soak' away from the heater.
iv)   Due consideration to the diversity of the workpieces to take into account contact arrangements (DRH) and coil configuration (IH) must be paid.
v)   If the workpiece 'diameter' is large a soaking period may be necessary (away from the induction heater) since the induction heating mechanism is via 'skin-effect'.

Where the student is asked to describe the instrumentation (as in the original examination question) reference might be made to arrangements based on electro-mechanical systems involving Trivectors. More appropriately electronic systems are now available.

Direct resistance heating

2.1. Background to the teaching

The topic covers those processes where a medium is heated directly by the passage of current through it. In turn this implies intimate contact between the medium or workpiece and the power source. The family of processes include:

Metal reheating for working and heat treatment.
Metallurgical extraction processes including the group of furnaces erroneously referred to as submerged arc furnaces.
Welding.
Glass melting, holding and refining.
Steam raising in electrode boilers.
Food processing.
Metal power sintering.

In its simplest form, the passage of direct current through simple conductors, two immediate constraints are met: heat losses from the work piece during heating and the need for a large ratio of workpiece length to the principal cross-section axis (diameter). Introducing alternating current flow through various geometries leads to two essential calculations, the nature and specification of the current source and the impedance presented to that source[14,15].

Most metal workpiece geometries lead to complex functions relating work piece impedance with frequency, geometry, resistivity, permeability (for magnetic workpieces) and any proximity to other conductors. The analysis may be presented as the relationship between the ratio of resistance at the relevant frequency to resistance for direct current against a term describing dimensional variations for standard workpiece geometries. For example, the resistance ratio may be plotted against the ratio of width to penetration depth for a flat sheet. A further complication is the dependence of resistivity (and permeability where relevant) on temperature as the workpiece heats up leading in turn to a significant change in skin depth. Firm connexions between the supply source and the workpiece have to be made to avoid further resistive losses at the clamps.

Direct resistance heating of metallic workpieces are discussed informatively by Davies[16].

The direct resistance heating of fluids is neglected in the literature. An elementary review of water heating and steam raising[17] refers to the empiricism of the subject and consideration of an electrode steam boiler does give rise to an unusual application of steam tables.

Other direct resistance processes are quite specialised, several involving metal, metal-slag, metal-slag-refractory reactions which do not lead to ready analysis. The electroslag remelting and welding processes are such[18]. A common situation met in many of these processes can be described by a little known property of 3-wire, 3-phase circuits whereby changes in the resistance in one phase have a considerable effect on the power and current in the previous phase, in the sequence of phase rotation, whereas the following phase is hardly affected[19].

In heating conductors the quantity of heat absorbed in a given volume is often required. This has led to the concept of volume specific heat, used by Davies[16] and others, denoted usually by $[C.\gamma]$ where C is specific heat $(J.kg^{-1}.K^{-1}]$ and $\gamma =$ density $[kgm^{-3}]$ so that the units of $[C.\gamma]$ are $J.m^{-3}.K^{-1}$. Thus for convenience some examples may be using C and γ or $[C.\gamma]$.

Most degree and diploma courses that consider this topic do so in an elementary way. This is to neglect some aspects which can be quite evolutionary in student development. For example the heating of magnetic wire or strip on the fly by alternating current can give an insight into the nature of electrical impedance denied by the conventional consideration of circuits currents and conductors.

Example DH1 in Chapter 5 may also be considered with the examples in this chapter.

Finally, those who wish to present 'low frequency' and 'high frequency' heating phenomena in the same course should consider using a unified theory approach where the displacement current appearing in Maxwell's equations can be emphasised (but never neglected!) according to the level of applied frequency[21].

2.2. The worked examples

DRH 1

Describe briefly an application of direct resistance heating in the metals industries.

What are the advantages of the process compared with any competitive heating process that could be envisaged for the chosen application?

A 25 m steel rod of diameter 10 mm is to be heated from 20 to 720 °C. Given a mean density of 7.85 tonnes/m³, a *mean* specific heat of 0.2 kWh/kg°C and a constant resistivity of 0.5×10^{-6} ohm.m, determine the dc supply needed to heat the rod in one minute.

In contrast a billet of the same steel of length 0.15 m and diameter 100 mm is to be heated in the same time. Again determine the dc supply required.

From your results what conclusions do you draw?

(*Extended from Reference 16*)

Solution

The word direct implies that current flows by direct contact between the supply source and the workpiece and the student would be expected to highlight simplicity, speed of heating and ease of control. An advantage compared with fossil fuel systems is usually reduced tonnage (inertia) of heated material in the processing line, improved environment and a rate of rise of temperature theoretically dictated only by the physical properties of the workpiece with consequent reduction in scale loss.

The dc supply for the 25 m rod

In the first instance, ignore losses due to radiation as the rod heats up.

Energy stored = temperature rise × volume × density × specific heat

$$= 700 \times \left[25 \times \frac{\pi}{4} \times \left[\frac{10}{1000} \right]^2 \right] \times 7.85 \times 0.2 \times 3.6 \times 10^6 \, \text{J}$$

$$= 7.77 \, \text{MJ}.$$

$$\text{Resistance} = \frac{\text{resistivity} \times \text{length}}{\text{area}} = \frac{0.5}{10^6} \times \frac{25}{\frac{\pi}{4} \times \left[\frac{10}{1000} \right]^2}$$

$$= 0.159 \, \text{ohms}.$$

$$\text{Energy} = I^2 . R . t$$

$$I^2 = \frac{7.77 \times 10^6}{0.159 \times 60}$$

$$I = 902 \, \text{amperes}$$

$$V = I . R = 902 \times 0.159$$

$$= 143 \, \text{volts}$$

Power delivered $= V . I = 129 \, \text{kW}$

The dc supply for the 0.25 m long billet

$$\text{Energy stored} = 700 \times \left[0.25 \times \frac{\pi}{4} \times \left[\frac{100}{1000} \right]^2 \right] \times 7.85 \times 0.2 \times 3.6 \times 10^6 \, \text{J}$$

Energy stored $\quad = 7.78 \, \text{MJ}$

$$\text{Resistance} = \frac{0.5}{10^6} \times \frac{0.25}{\dfrac{\pi}{4} \times \left[\dfrac{100}{1000} \right]^2}$$

$$= 1.59 \times 10^{-5} \, \text{ohm}$$

$$I^2 = \frac{7.78 \times 10^6}{1.59 \times 10^{-5}} \times 60$$

$$I = 90{,}262 \, \text{amperes}$$

$$V = 90{,}262 \times 1.59 \times 10^{-5}$$

$$= 1.44 \, \text{volts}$$

Power delivered $= 129.5 \, \text{kW}$

It should be concluded that the second case is not a candidate for direct resistance heating. Although the energy power requirements are the same it requires high currents and very low applied voltages. Contact losses and $i^2 R$ losses in the source circuit would be prohibitively high.

DRH2

Repeat DRH1 for copper taking $(C\gamma) = 3.66 \times 10^6 \, \text{Jm}^{-3}\text{K}^{-1}$ and $\rho = 0.042 \times 10^{-6} \, \text{ohm.metre}$. Draw some conclusions.

(Reference 16)

Solution
Taking the presentation adopted in the second part of DRM1 then:

For the 25 m rod:

$$\text{Energy stored} = 700 \times \left[25 \times \frac{\pi}{4} \times \left(\frac{10}{1000} \right)^2 \right] \times 3.66 \times 10^6 \, \text{J}$$

$$= 5.03 \, \text{MJ}$$

$$\text{Resistance} = \frac{0.042 \times 10^{-6} \times 25}{\dfrac{\pi}{4} \times \left[\dfrac{10}{1000} \right]^2}$$

$$= 0.0134 \, \text{ohms}$$

$$I^2 = \frac{5.03 \times 10^6}{0.0134 \times 60}$$

$$I = 2,500 \text{ amperes}$$

$$V = 2,500 \times 0.0134$$

$$= 33.5 \text{ volts}$$

Power required $= 83.9 \text{ kW}$

For the 0.25 m billet:
Energy stored $= 5.03 \text{ MJ}$ as before

$$\text{Resistance} = \frac{0.042 \times 10^{-6} \times 0.25}{\frac{\pi}{4} \times \left[\frac{100}{1000}\right]^2}$$

$$= 1.34 \times 10^{-6} \text{ ohms}$$

$$I^2 = \frac{5.03 \times 10^6}{1.34 \times 10^{-6} \times 60}$$

$$I = 250,000 \text{ amperes}$$

$$V = 250,000 \times 1.34 \times 10^{-6}$$

$$= 0.335 \text{ volts}$$

Power required $= 0.335 \times 250,000$

$$= 83.8 \text{ kW}$$

The comparison of steel with copper shows that in both cases the currents are higher and the voltages lower. In the case of the 0.25 m billet it would be impossible to use direct resistance heating effectively.

DRH3

i) A steel billet 2 m long and 100 mm in diameter is to be heated using direct resistance heating from 10 °C to 1250 °C in 120 seconds. Find the constant current required to achieve this assuming the total losses during the cycle are equal to 10% of the energy needed to heat the billet.

   Given: Density $= 7.85$ tonnes/m^3
   Average specific heat $= 0.2$ kWh/kg°C
   Resistivity at 10°C $= 0.1 \times 10^{-6}$ ohm.m
   Resistivity at 1250 °C $= 1.22 \times 10^{-6}$ ohm.m

   Discuss the influence of using 50 Hz compared with dc.

ii) If power factor is found to vary between 0.6 to 0.85 for the heating circuit estimate the plant rating and the range of output voltages if the process is conducted at constant current.

iii) If the throughput is to be 4 tonnes per hour and the handling time for each billet is 60 seconds determine the new power supply (based on constant current throughout the cycle).

(After Reference 6, with modifications)

Solution

Discussion   Most examples will use dc for simplicity. In this case some reference to alternating current systems is required. In induction heating, resistance change over a temperature range can be accommodated to a first approximation using the concept of integrated resistivity (reference 20 p22). In this case skin depth (referred to the semi-infinite slab situation) will vary from 20 mm to about 80 mm.

The power density (loss) per square metre of surface area

$$= \frac{\rho \hat{J}^2}{4} \cdot \delta$$

where $\hat{J}$ is the peak *surface* current, ρ resistivity and δ skin depth.

Clearly the current distribution will be more symmetrical for the billet the higher the temperature but the *surface* current will be dictated by the supply voltage. Thus the concept of constant current referred to *must* in real situations be treated with caution. With the low temperature case a value of surface current greater than the mean current must be provided with an associated higher supplied voltage. For copper workpieces over the temperature range the skin depth (referred to the semi-infinite slab situation) varies more modestly (about 22–30 m.m) and in practical calculations is neglected.

Fortunately, as will be seen, the concept of constant current requires a variable voltage which, for dc, requires a higher voltage at the higher temperature to accommodate the radical change in resistivity.

The example will be worked out assuming a dc supply with appropriate guidance to cover the ac case.

Part (i)

$$\text{Heat required for the billet} = \frac{\pi}{4} \times \left(\frac{100}{1000}\right)^2 \times 2 \times 7.85 \times 10^3 \times 0.2 \times 1240$$

$$= 30.58 \, \text{kWh}$$

$$\text{Total heat required} = 30.58 \times 1.1$$

$$= 33.64 \, \text{kWh}$$

$$\text{Power required} = 33.64 \times \frac{60 \times 60}{120}$$

$$= 1 \, \text{MW}$$

If the mean resistivity of 0.66×10^{-6} ohm.m is assumed

$$\text{Then resistance} = \frac{0.66 \times 10^{-6} \times 2}{\frac{\pi}{4} \times \left(\frac{100}{1000}\right)^2}$$

$$= 1.68 \times 10^{-4} \, \text{ohms.}$$

$$\text{and the current} = \left[\frac{10^6}{1.68} \times 10^{-4}\right]^{1/2}$$

$$= 77.5 \, \text{kA.}$$

Observation: at this stage the influence that this choice of current may have in achieving the required power is not required.

There are two possible routes for the ac case.

a) The integrated resistivity for the range (reference 20 p22)

$$= \frac{[\sqrt{1.22 \times 10^{-6}} + \sqrt{0.1 \times 10^{-6}}]^2}{4}$$

$$= 0.505 \times 10^{-6} \, \text{ohm.m.}$$

$$\text{Heat required for the billet} = \frac{\pi}{4} \times \left(\frac{100}{1000}\right)^2 \times 2 \times 7.85 \times 10^3 \times 0.2 \times 1240$$

$$= 30.58 \, \text{kWh.}$$

$$\text{Total heat required} = 30.58 \times 1.1$$

$$= 33.64 \, \text{kWh}$$

$$\text{Power required} = 33.64 \times \frac{60 \times 60}{120}$$

$$= 1\,\text{MW}$$

$$\text{Resistance} = \frac{0.505 \times 10^{-6} \times 2}{\frac{\pi}{4} \times \left(\frac{100}{1000}\right)^2}$$

$$= 1.29 \times 10^{-4}\,\text{ohms}$$

$$\text{Constant current} = \left[\frac{1 \times 10^6}{1.29 \times 10^{-4}}\right]^{1/2}$$

$$= 88{,}000\,\text{amperes}$$

b) Simply assume that the 'average' resistivity is 0.66 $\times 10^{-6}$ ohm.m.

which produces a constant current of 77.5 kA. This is *also* the only solution readily applicable to dc.

Clearly a view has to be taken of the influence of skin effect (the phenomenon would not occur with dc) and perhaps the weighting of radiation losses as temperature increases. In this example skin depth for steel varies from 20 mm to 79 mm but there is little difference between the dc and the ac cases at temperature since the ten-fold increase in resistivity masks the four-fold increase in skin depth with an associated increase in achievable power density if constant current is maintained.

Part (ii)

The conditions at the start and the completion of the cycle need to be compared to determine the maximum rating.

$$\text{Resistance at the start} = \frac{(0.1 \times 10^{-6}) \times 2}{\frac{\pi}{4} \times (10 \times 10^{-2})^2}$$

$$= 2.55 \times 10^{-5}\,\text{ohm.}$$

$$\text{Power developed} = (77.5 \times 10^3)^2 \times (2.55 \times 10^{-5}) \times 10^{-3}$$

[the lower solution of current is used to ensure full range covered]

$$= 153\,\text{kW}$$

$$\text{kVA required} = \frac{153}{0.6} = 255$$

$$\text{Voltage required} = \frac{255}{77.5} = 3.29\,\text{volts}$$

$$\text{Resistance at the end} = \frac{(1.22 \times 10^{-6}) \times 2}{\frac{\pi}{4} \times (10 \times 10^{-2})^2} \quad \text{(ignoring expansion)}$$

$$= 3.11 \times 10^{-4} \, \text{ohm}$$

$$\text{kVA required} = \frac{(88.0 \times 10^3)^2 \times 3.11 \times 10^{-4} \times 10^{-3}}{0.85}$$

using the upper solution of current

$$= 2830 \, \text{kVa}$$

$$\text{Voltage required} = \frac{2830}{88} = 32.2 \, \text{volts}$$

Thus a voltage range of 32.5 to 3.25 and a rating of 3.0 MVA†
would be chosen.

Part (iii)

The weight of a billet

$$= \frac{\pi}{4} \times (10 \times 10^{-2})^2 \times 2 \times 7.85$$

$$= 0.123 \, \text{tonnes.}$$

$$\text{Number of billets heated per hour} = \frac{4}{0.123} = 32.4$$

$$\text{Time for each billet} = \frac{3600}{32.4}$$

$$= 111 \, \text{seconds}$$

Time available for heating $= 111 - 60 = 51$ seconds.

$$\text{Thus the power required} = \frac{30.58 \times 3600}{51}$$

(the radiation losses are
neglected bearing in mind
the rapid heating time)

$$= 2154 \, \text{kW}$$

$$\text{with a 'constant' current} = \left(\frac{2154 \times 10^3}{1.29 \times 10^{-4}}\right)^{1/2}$$

$$= 129 \, \text{kA}$$

---

†If the constant value of current of 77.5 kiloamps is chosen then the rating reduces
to 2.2 MVA and the upper voltage to 28.5 V.

DRH4

An industrial direct resistance heater, using 50 Hz, consists of a single phase transformer with a simple go and return conductor arrangement. One conductor is of copper, the other, the workpiece, is steel. If both conductors are of the same radius r and are separated by a distance D, by using the approximate relationship

$$L = \frac{\mu_r . \mu_0}{\pi} . ln\left[\frac{D}{r}\right] \text{H/m} \quad \text{or otherwise}$$

show that the ratio of the incremental change in reactance to the incremental change in resistance is given by the relation:

$$\frac{\frac{\delta L}{L}}{\frac{\delta R}{R}} \rightarrow \frac{1}{2 . ln\left[\dfrac{D}{r}\right]}$$

An alloy steel bar of diameter 0.075 m with a separation distance from a direct-resistance heater "go" conductor of copper of 0.75 m is linked to a 50 Hz transformer. Calculate the transformer rating if a 1 metre bar is to be heated in one minute to a temperature of 1230 °C above ambient.

The cost of such an alternating current unit is expressed by the term $[10 + (0.038 \times kVA)] \times 10^3$ in pounds sterling. With rectification or to supply a comparable power by direct current the expression is £$[50 + (0.035 \times kVA)] \times 10^3$. What must the length of the bar be to justify the use of direct current?

Take average resistivity of steel as 1×10^{-6} ohm-m, the density of the steel as 7,500 kg/m^3, its average specific heat as 420 J/kgK. The steel is non-magnetic so $\mu_r = 1$ and $\mu_0 = 4\pi \times 10^{-1}$ H/m.

(From Electroheat Tutorials, Cambridge University)

Solution

$$\text{Taking } L = \frac{\mu_r . \mu_0}{\pi} . ln\frac{D}{r}$$

$$\text{Then } \frac{1}{L} . \frac{dL}{dr} = \frac{1}{L} . \frac{\mu_r . \mu_0}{\pi} . \frac{1}{r}$$

$$= \frac{1}{r . ln[D/r]}$$

The resistance R per unit length is:

$$R = \frac{\rho}{\pi \cdot r^2}$$

$$\therefore \quad \frac{dR}{dr} = \frac{-2\rho}{\pi r^3}$$

$$\text{or} \quad \frac{1}{R} \cdot \frac{dR}{dr} = \frac{-2}{r}$$

$\therefore$ the ratio of the incremental change of reactance to the incremental change of resistance is derived from:

$$\frac{\dfrac{1}{L} \cdot \dfrac{dL}{dr}}{\dfrac{1}{R} \cdot \dfrac{dR}{dr}} = \frac{1}{2 \, ln \left[\dfrac{D}{r} \right]} \quad \ldots \ldots \text{ QED}$$

Ignoring copper and radiation losses:

$$\text{Then heat required for the bar} = \frac{\pi \times 0.075^2}{4} \times 1 \times 7,500 \times \frac{420}{3,600} \times \frac{1,230}{1,000}$$

$$= 4.755 \, kWh$$

$$\text{Power required} = 4.755 \times 60$$

$$= 285 \, kW$$

$$\text{Resistance of bar} = \frac{10^{-6} \times 4}{\pi \times 0.075^2}$$

$$= 2.26 \times 10^{-4} \, \text{ohms}$$

$$\text{Reactance of secondary circuit} = \frac{2 \times \pi \times 50}{\pi} \times 4\pi \times 10^{-7} \, ln \left[\frac{0.75 \times 2}{0.075} \right]$$

$$= 3.76 \, \text{ohms}$$

$$\text{Power factor (cos } \phi) = 0.515$$

$$\therefore \quad \text{rating of transformer} = 553 \, kVA$$

For parity of direct and alternating current supplied and Z the length of the bar

$$\left[\frac{10 + 0.038 \times kW \times Z}{\cos \phi} \right] = [50 + 0.035 \times kW \times Z]$$

$$\text{giving } Z = 3.62 \text{ metres}$$

$$\text{(say 4 metres)}$$

DRH5

A flat sheet of steel is to be heated from $900\,^{\circ}$C to $1100\,^{\circ}$C in a warm rolling process between roll passes. Given $\rho_{900} = 1.135 \times 10^{-6}$, $\sigma_{1100} = 1.195 \times 10^{-6}\,\Omega$m and $(c\gamma)$ as contant at $5.9 \times 10^6\,\mathrm{Wsm^{-3}K^{-1}}$, find the working depth of penetration at 50 Hz. If the sheet is 5.0 mm thick, 1 m wide and the distance between the contacts is 4 m, ignore losses, find the power required to heat the sheet in 20 seconds. Hence comment on this application.

(*Electroheat Tutorials — the author*)

Solution

$$\delta = \sqrt{\frac{2 \times 1.165 \times 10^{-6}}{1 \times 4\pi \times 10^{-7} \times 2\pi \times 50}}$$

$$= 76.8\,\mathrm{mm}$$

$$\text{Energy stored} = 200 \times (0.005 \times 1 \times 4) \times 5.9 \times 10^6$$

$$= 23.6\,\mathrm{MJ}$$

$$\text{Resistance} = 1.165 \times 10^{-6} \times \frac{4}{0.005} \times \Gamma \quad \text{Now } \frac{b}{\delta} = \frac{2.5}{76.8} < 1$$

$$= 9.32 \times 10^{-4}\,\Omega \qquad \text{and } \frac{R_{ac}}{R_{dc}} = 1.0\ [=\Gamma]$$

$$I^2 = \frac{23.6 \times 10^6}{9.32 \times 10^{-4} \times 20} = 0.1266 \times 10^{10}$$

$$I = 0.356 \times 10^5 = 35.6\,\mathrm{kA}$$

$$V = 35.6 \times 10^3 \times 9.32 \times 10^{-4}$$

$$= 33.16\,\mathrm{V}$$

$$\therefore \quad P = 33.26 \times 35.6 \times 10^3$$

$$= 1.18\,\mathrm{MW}$$

Comment

Needs an awful lot of power and 20 seconds is a modest process time. Therefore if on-line, the warm rolling process is relatively slow.

DRH6

Show that the current density in a directly heated metallic rectangular slab of total height 2b, width w and surface current density J_s is given by

$$\hat{J}_x(y) = J_s \frac{\cosh(1+j)y/\delta}{\cosh(1+j)b/\delta}$$

Integrate between limits $-b$ and $+b$ to find the total current flow and hence show that the ac resistance exceeds the dc resistance by the factor

$$(b/\delta).\left(\sinh\frac{2b}{\delta} + \sin\frac{2b}{\delta}\right)\bigg/\left(\cosh\frac{2b}{\delta} - \cos\frac{2b}{\delta}\right)$$

where δ is the skin depth. Calculate this factor for a 100 mm slab of aluminium at 50 Hz given that $\rho = 5.7 \times 10^{-8}\,\Omega\text{m}$, $\mu_r = 1$.

(Electroheat Tutorials — the author)

Solution
The analysis may be deduced from several sources for example reference 14 pages 209–211.

Then starting from (equation 8.43 from 14):

$$R_{ac} = R_{dc}.\frac{b}{\delta}.\left(\sinh\frac{2b}{\delta} + \sin\frac{2b}{\delta}\right)\bigg/\left(\cosh\frac{2b}{\delta} - \cos\frac{2b}{\delta}\right)$$

$$\delta = \sqrt{\frac{2}{\sigma.\mu_r.\mu_o.\omega}} = \sqrt{\frac{2 \times 5.7 \times 10^{-8}}{4\pi.10^{-7}.2.\pi.50}}$$

$$= 0.0170\,\text{m}$$

but $\qquad 2b = 100\,\text{mm}$

$$\therefore \quad \frac{b}{\delta} = \frac{50 \times 10^{-3}}{0.0170} \left[\text{and } \frac{2b}{\delta} = 5.882\right]$$

$$= 2.9412$$

$$\sinh\frac{2b}{\delta} = 179.26; \quad \sin\frac{2b}{\delta} = -0.3902$$

$$\cosh\frac{2b}{\delta} = 179.26; \quad \cos\frac{2b}{\delta} = 0.9206$$

$$\therefore \text{ the required factor is } \frac{R_{ac}}{R_{dc}} = 2.92$$

DRH7

a) Explain why the ac resistance of a conductor is higher than its dc resistance.

b) A steel tube with external and internal diameters of 3 cm and 2.4 cm respectively is to be used as a heating element by passing 50 Hz current through it. The steel tube is required to provide 5 kW of background heating to a commercial greenhouse over a length of 100 m. The following data have been provided with the tube.

Current (A)	$k = \dfrac{\text{ac resistance at } 20°C}{\text{dc resistance at } 20°C}$	Steady state temperature rise above ambient of 20°C $\Delta\theta°C$
90	4.31	27
120	3.84	43
140	3.61	55
160	3.42	68
200	3.13	95

If the resistivity of steel is 15.6×10^{-8} Ω-m at 20 °C and the temperature coefficient of resistance over the temperature range considered is 44×10^{-4} per °C at 20 °C calculate for an estimated operating power factor of 0.93 lag:

i) the required current at the operating temperature to generate 5 kW in the tube,

ii) the kVA rating of the transformer,

iii) the transformer secondary voltage required.

(Courtesy of NELP (B.Sc Final 1985))
(See also example IRH10 and the background to the teaching in Chapter 3)

Solution

The student would be expected to review the influence of short lengths, the ratio length/cross sectional area, irregular shapes (including non-uniform cross sectional area) with a discussion of skin effect.

The resistance at 20 °C is given by:

$$R_{20} = \frac{15.6 \times 10^{-8}}{\pi.[1.5^2 - 1.2^2] \times 10^{-4}}$$

$$= 6.13 \times 10^{-4} \text{ ohms per metre.}$$

The data can be used to tabulate current and the expected power dissipation at 20 °C from Power $= I^2 R_{ac}$.

Current kA	k	Calculated power at 20°C W.m^{-1}	$\Delta\theta$°C
90	4.31	21.4	27
120	3.84	33.9	43
140	3.61	43.4	55
160	3.42	53.7	68
200	3.13	76.8	95

These are plotted on figure DRH7.

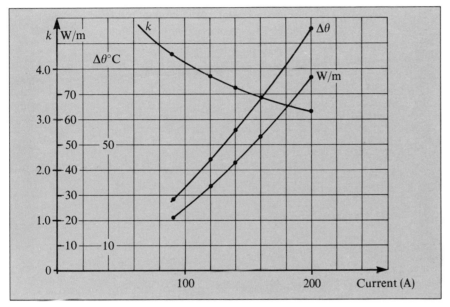

Figure DRH7

For 5 kW to be supplied at 20 °C this will require an instantaneous
current of 154 A (from the graph). If 154 A is maintained a
temperature rise of 63 °C occurs (i.e. 83 °C). The dc resistance at
83°C is given by:

$$R_{83} = 6.13 \times 10^{-4}(1 + 44.0 \times 10^{-4} \times 63)$$

$$= 7.83 \times 10^{-4} \text{ ohms per metre.}$$

and at $\Delta\theta = 63$ °C, $K = 3.5$

$$\therefore \quad \text{operating current} = \sqrt{\frac{50}{3.5 \times 7.83 \times 10^{-4}}} = 135.0 \text{ A}$$

Now the supply transformer must be capable of supplying 5 kW
throughout the temperature range. If the supply voltage at
temperature is first calculated:

then $\text{kV.A} = \dfrac{5.0}{0.93} = 5.38$ at temperature

$$V = \frac{5000}{135 \times 93} = 39.82 \text{ volts and this is the required}$$

secondary voltage.

The transformer must supply a maximum of $\dfrac{39.82 \times 154}{0.93} = 6.59\,\text{kVA}$

at $20\,°C$ (ignoring transformer regulation).

DRH8

List four advantages and four disadvantages of direct resistance billet heating and state the conditions under which maximum efficiency can be achieved.

A mineral insulated metal sheathed immersion heater is to be designed to heat the fuel oil supplying a boiler. The flow rate is 150 lt/hr and the immersion heater has to raise the temperature of the oil by 45°C. The heating element is to be formed in a helix of 5 mm internal diameter with a ratio of pitch to wire diameter of 2. The surface power density for the heating element must not exceed $37\,\text{kW/m}^2$ and for the metal sheath $15\,\text{kW/m}^2$. For a supply voltage of 240 V and a heating element resistance of $0.75\,\Omega/\text{m}$ calculate:

a)   the power rating of the immersion heater,

b)   the length and diameter of the heating element wire,

c)   the number of turns of the heating element,

d)   the length and diameter of the metal sheath.

The specific heat of oil is $2100\,\text{J}\,\text{kg}^{-1}\,\text{K}^{-1}$ and its density $900\,\text{kg}\,\text{m}^{-3}$.

(Courtesy of NELP (B.Sc. Finals 1982))

Solution
The advantages might cover yield improvement (rapid heating leads to low scale loss), high efficiency (for steel), low capital cost compared with induction heating (when comparable), easy application of automatic control, easy control of production schedules, no need to hold billets at temperature (therefore reduced stand-by losses), temperature profiling is possible which can lead to low wear levels on tools and dies.

The disadvantages include product restriction to the ratio length/'diameter' > 6, contact problems of stock to heater and temperature shadowing at the contacts, power factor correction with ac is required, there are difficulties in heating non-uniform cross sections, particularly axially, non-ferrous workpieces are heated inefficiently and with large systems phase balancing may be required.

To obtain efficient heating the resistance of the workpiece should be an order greater than the transformer's (source) impedance and the ratio length/'diameter' should be greater than 20. The short heating times required to achieve high efficiency infer the use of high currents with attendant contact problems.

NOTE: The rest of this example should appear with the examples given in Chapter 3.

The power rating of the immersion heating (kW)

$$= \text{(flow rate in cubic metres per second)} \times \text{(density)}$$
$$\times \text{(specific heat)} \times \text{temperature rise)}$$

$$= \frac{150 \times 1000 \times 10^{-6} \times 900 \times 2100 \times 45}{3600} \times 10^{-3}$$

$$= 3.54$$

Again the required heater resistance $= \dfrac{240^2}{3.54 \times 10^3}$ ohms

and the element length $= \dfrac{240^2}{3.54 \times 10^3 \times 0.75} = 21.7$ metres

and its diameter $= \dfrac{3.54 \times 10^3}{\pi \times 21.7 \times 37,000}$

$$= 1.4 \times 10^{-3} \text{ metres } (1.4 \text{ mm})$$

The mean diameter of the turns of the element $= (5 + 1.4)$ mm

$$\therefore \quad \text{number of turns} = \frac{21.7}{\pi[6.4].10^{-3}} = 1080$$

The helix length $= 2 \times 1.4 \times 10^{-3} \times 1080 = 3.02$ m

with a small end clearance this gives a sheath length of 3.07 m (say).

The diameter of the sheath $= \dfrac{3540}{\pi \times 3.07 \times 15,000} = 24.5$ mm.

DRH9

a) Explain why

    i)   the resistance of a billet to an alternating current is larger than to an equal magnitude direct current.

    ii)   the power factor of a billet heater varies during the heating cycle and is dependent on the diameter of the billet.

b) Steel rods with a diameter of 2 cm and length 60 cm are to be heated to 420 °C by a direct resistance heater at the rate of 70 per hour with a handling time of 12 sec. A constant current operation is required and the estimated power factor at the start of the heating cycle is 0.6 and after 10 sec. 0.9. If the ratio of $\dfrac{\text{resistance to alternating current}}{\text{resistance to direct current}} \dfrac{(R_{ac})}{(R_{dc})}$ at 20 °C varies as shown in Figure DRH11/1 and R_{ac} increases by a factor of 5 after 10 sec., calculate the transformer secondary voltages. Average heat losses can be taken at 5% of the power requirement.

Physical properties of the steel are

                Average specific heat   720 J/kgK

                Resistivity at 20°C $15 \times 10^{-8}\,\Omega\text{m}$

                Density $8 \times 10^{3}\,\text{kg/m}^{3}$

(Courtesy of NELP (B.Sc. Finals 1983))

Solution

a)   Reference can be made to earlier examples as well as Hammond[14] and Davies[16].

i)   heating $= \dfrac{3600 - 70 \times 12}{70} = 39.4$ sec. for each billet.

Resistance of each billet at 20 °C is

$$R_{20} = \frac{15 \times 10^{-8} \times 60 \times 10^{-2} \times 4}{\pi \times 10^{-4} \times 2^{2}}$$

$$= 286 \times 10^{-6}\,\Omega\text{m}$$

Power required $= \dfrac{720 \times \pi \times 2^{2} \times 10^{-4} \times 60 \times 10^{-2} \times 8 \times 10^{3}}{4 \times 39.4} \times (420 - 20)$

and since losses are 5% of 11,000 (= 550 W)

Power supplied = 11.55 kW

Using figure DRH9/1 the following table can be constructed.

I (kA)	K	$R_{\text{eff}} = K \times R_{\text{dc}}(\Omega)$	$P = I^2 R_{eff}(\text{kW})$
1	4.25	1215	1.21
2	3.2	915	3.66
3	2.55	729	6.56
4	2.4	606	10.98
5	2.2	629	15.7
6	2.15	615	22.1
7	2.1	600	29.4

Figure DRH9/2 can now be plotted.

At start-up

$$\text{kVA} = \frac{11.55}{0.6} = 19.25$$

and from figure DRH9/2 the current is 4.2 kA which is to be kept constant so that at start-up the transformer secondary voltage

$$= \frac{19.250}{4.2} = 4.58 \text{ V.}$$

After 10 seconds the power factor is 0.9, the new power $= 55 + \text{losses}$ $= 57.75 \text{ kW}$ and $\text{kVA} = 57.75/0.9 = 64.17$.

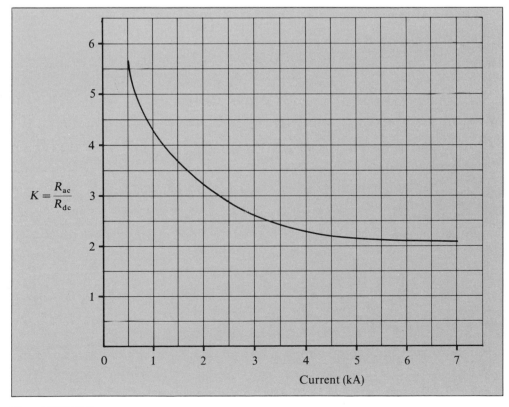

Figure DRH9/1

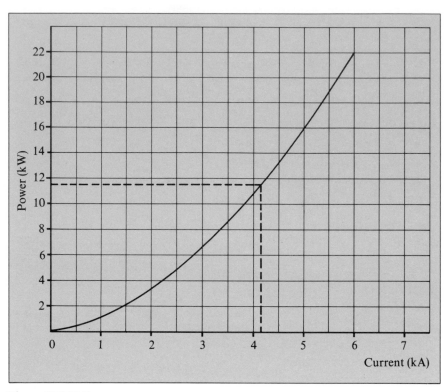

Figure DRH 9/2

So the new transformer terminal voltage $= 64.17/4.2$

$$= 15.3 \text{ volts}$$

Thus the required voltage range is from 4.6 to 15.3 volts.

DRH10

Describe the process of electrolysis as a direct current flows through an electrolyte and explain how the passage of an alternating current would modify the process.

It is required to generate 2520 kg/h of dry steam at 5 bar, using a 415 V, 3-phase electrode boiler of 97% thermal efficiency. Feedwater is at 20 °C, and the electrode current density limit of 2.5 kA/m² must be observed. What is the minimum theoretical electrode area required?

Discuss what practical factors might affect the actual area chosen, compared with the theoretical indication.

[*after reference 17*]

Solution

A brief description found in any good appropriate text book would suffice. With alternating current the essential feature to observe is that the polarisation and deposition phenomena disappear and essentially a thermal effect remains. As power density increases so the rate of rise of temperature leads to the concept of an electrode boiler using water as a medium for heating water or producing steam. With dc gas evolution will take place at each electrode and this evolution is not lost until a frequency of about 10 Hz is reached. Certainly for 50 Hz there are few gasification problems. Treating the electrolyte as a dielectric again a breakdown of resistance will occur at radio-frequencies but this is not a practical problem. The important limits of voltage are set at the lower end by a level sufficient to permit adequate power absorbtion and at the upper limit by electrolyte collapse at which levels damage to electrodes can occur. Empirically, a maximum voltage gradient of 25 kV/m is used which in turn is related to electrode geometry and spacing.

Steam tables give the enthalpy of dry steam at 5 bar as 2,749 kJ/kg, and of water at 20 °C as 83.9 kJ/kg.

Net enthalpy input required $= 2749 - 83.9 = 2665.1$ kJ/kg

At 97% efficiency,
Gross input required $= \dfrac{2665.1}{0.97} = 2747.5$ kJ/kg

The flow of dry steam $= \dfrac{2520}{3600} = 0.7$ kg/s

and the input power $= 2747.5 \times 0.7 = 193.3 \dfrac{kJ}{s}$ (or kW)

At maximum current density,
electrode energy density $= 2.5$ kA/m$^2 \times 415$ V $\times \sqrt{3}$

$= 1797$ kW/m^2

Minimum electrode area $= \dfrac{1923.3}{1797} = 1.07$ m^2

In practice, one must ask whether all the electrode area will be available as immersed area, what allowance need be made for the effects of scaling, whether water conductivity can be controlled to ensure that the design current can always be drawn when required and what 'next size up' standard product is available.

DRH11

An electrode boiler is to be used to produce dry steam continuously at a rate of 10,000 kg per hour at a pressure of 550 kN/m². The design of the boiler is such that it is equivalent to a concentric cylinder arrangement with the inner and outer cylinders being the two electrodes; they have diameters of 200 mm and 1 m respectively. The height of the electrodes, which are completely immersed in water during operation, is 1 m. Calculate the total power requirement and the voltage applied to the electrodes. Take the temperature of the feed water as 0 °C.

(Take limiting field strength as 25 V/mm, and current density as 2.5 kA/m².)

Solution
Enthalpy = 2753 kJ/kg (from tables)

Area of inner electrode $= 2.\pi.r.l = 2 \times \pi \times 0.1 \times 1.0$

$$= 0.628 \, \text{m}^2$$

Energy required/hour = flow rate × enthalpy = $10,000 \times 2753$ kJ

Energy required/second $= \dfrac{10,000 \times 2753}{3600} \, \text{kW}$

$$= 7.65 \, \text{MW}$$

If used to maximum current density

$$\text{Current} = 2.5 \times 0.628 \, \text{kA}$$

$$= 1570 \, \text{A}$$

$$\text{and Voltage} \doteqdot \frac{7.65 \times 10^6}{1.560 \times 10^3} = 4.9 \, \text{kV}$$

Distance between electrodes is 40 cm and voltage gradient
$$= \frac{4.9}{400} \times 10^3 = 12.25 \, \text{V/mm}.$$

Maximum permissible voltage $= 25 \times 400 = 10 \, \text{kV}$

$\therefore$ design is acceptable.

Indirect resistance heating

3.1. Background to the teaching

Indirect resistance heating invariably requires the use of a resistance element which produces heat which is transferred to the workpiece. Where the element is the thermal energy source in an oven or furnace radiation and convection are the principle heat transfer mechanisms, where the element is in contact with the workpiece conduction is the principle mechanism.

Perhaps this heating process is numerically the largest in terms of individual loads in the industrial electrical heating sector, with the most diverse applications, yet, if it is taught formally at all, the presentation leaves much to be desired. Harry[22] approaches the topic methodically by reviewing the behaviour of electrical resistance and resistivity with temperature followed by an empirical reference to heat transfer mechanisms, control aspects, the application of radiation in ovens and furnaces and a copious reference to practical situations. Horsley[23] in the same source reviews heat transfer summarily. Nevertheless one is left feeling the topic needs a more sympathetic approach which has yet to be developed.

There are now several good undergraduate textbooks on Heat Transfer, any of which will no doubt have adherents. Usually there will be an adequate review of for example radiation[24]. It will refer to but not derive Planck's law, Wiens displacement law will be quoted and perhaps the Stefan-Boltzman equation derived (see example IRH4 below). Often a table of surface emissivities due to Hottel[25] will be given and tables of radiation functions and more practically based physical data quoted. The student will be faced with a degree of empiricism which in turn makes the design of worked examples tortuous and difficult for the setting of examinable material. The result of this approach is the neglect of an important area of work.

An elementary review of unsheathed and sheathed electric heating elements has been made[26,27] and from time to time practical guidelines are published demonstrating the flexible application of indirect resistance heating[28,29]. From the same source as references 28 and 29 is a brief review of industrial infra-red processes[30] which is useful in suggesting process classification and the individual status of critical technical parameters such as wavelength and power density.

Most of the worked examples which follow arise from the various quoted sources and have been used in at least two undergraduate courses. Reference may be made to certain specialised books of which Gray and Müller[31] is particularly helpful for radiative heat transfer and Chantry[32] for an up-to-date theoretical review from an unusual source.

Examples IRH10 and DRH7 have a common interest. The techniques of heating pipe lines carrying fluids at widely varying ambient temperatures[33,34,35] include the use of steel tubes and heating tapes wrapped around the pipe. These two examples provide an opportunity for a comparison of two techniques to be made. The use of steel saddle tubes is by no means elementary. Even the limited temperature range can cause significant changes in key material properties' phenomena which are under contemporary investigation[36,37].

Example DRH8 in Chapter 2 is also relevant to this chapter.

3.2. The worked examples

IRH1

A pipe of outside diameter 85 mm carries a fluid at 60 °C. It is intended to maintain this temperature by lagging the pipe with a spirally wound element around a lagging of 25 mm thickness insulation of thermal conductivity 0.052 W/mK. Determine the power required per metre run of pipe. The ambient temperature is 15 °C.

[*Modified from references 22 and 3.*]

Solution
The Fourier heat flow equation in radial form is:

$$q = -k.2.\pi.\frac{d\theta}{dr}$$

k is active thermal conductivity

q is heat flow in watts

$\frac{d\theta}{dr}$ is the temperature gradient

r is the active radius

θ is the temperature

Thus for the cylinder of insulation, internal radius r_1 external radius r_2, the temperature at r_1 is θ_1 and at r_2, θ_2 then:

$$q = -k.2\pi. \int_{\theta_1}^{\theta_2} d\theta \bigg/ \int_{r_1}^{r_2} \frac{dr}{r}$$

$$= -\frac{k.2\pi[\theta_2 - \theta_1]}{\ln[r_2/r_1]}$$

$$\therefore \quad \text{heatflow} = \frac{0.052.2\pi.[15 - 60]}{\ln[67.5/42.5]}$$

$$= -31.8 \text{ watts/metre and this is}$$
the power required to maintain
the liquid temperature by the
spirally wound element.

IRH2

Derive an expression relating the thermal radiation exchange between two long parallel surfaces each with zero transmissivity.

An infra-red emitter is required to stove paint on a flat surface. The optimum absorptivity (α) of a paint (0.6) occurs when the monochromatic power density is a maximum at $2.63\,\mu m$. To achieve the appropriate amount of stoving $36\,kW/m^2$ of total power is required. Consider the emitter and the paint surface to be long parallel surfaces, also consider the paint to be at ambient temperature $20\,°C$. Calculate the emissivity of the emitter.

Wein's displacement law is $\lambda_{max}.T = 289.6\,\mu mK$ and the Stefan-Boltzmann constant $= 5.669 \times 10^{-8}\,J/m^2.s.K$.

(Electroheat Tutorial, Aston University)

Solution

Let there be two surfaces, subscripts 1 and 2 respectively. The radiation from the first surface per unit area will be:

$\varepsilon_1.\sigma.\theta_1^4$ where ε is emissivity

         σ is the Stefan-Boltzmann constant with a value of $5.669 \times 10^{-8}\,J/m^2.s.K$.

         θ is temperature.

This will impinge on the second surface and an amount $\varepsilon_2.\varepsilon_1.\sigma.\theta_1^4$ is absorbed. The amount not absorbed, $(1-\varepsilon_2).\varepsilon_1.\sigma.\theta_1^4$ is reflected back to surface 1 which will absorb $\varepsilon_1.(1-\varepsilon_2).\varepsilon_1.\sigma.\theta_1^4$ and reflect $(1-\varepsilon_1).(1-\varepsilon_2).\varepsilon_1.\sigma.\theta_1^4$. Of this last surface 2 will absorb $\varepsilon_2.(1-\varepsilon_1).(1-\varepsilon_2).\varepsilon_1.\sigma.\theta_1^4$. As this process continues an expression can be built up for total power q_{12} watts absorbed per unit area of surface 1 such that

$$q_{1,2} = \varepsilon_2.\varepsilon_1.\sigma.\theta_1^4 + \varepsilon_2.\varepsilon_1.(1-\varepsilon_1).(1-\varepsilon_2).\sigma.\theta_1^4$$

$$+ \varepsilon_2.\varepsilon_1.(1-\varepsilon_1).(1-\varepsilon_2).(1-\varepsilon_1).(1-\varepsilon_2).\sigma.\theta_1^4 + \dots$$

$$+ \varepsilon_2.\varepsilon_1.(1-\varepsilon_1)^n.(1-\varepsilon_2)^n.\sigma.\theta_1^4$$

or for the total area A

$$q_{1,2} = \frac{A.\varepsilon_1.\varepsilon_2.\sigma.\theta_1{}^4}{[1-(1-\varepsilon_1).(1-\varepsilon_2)]}$$

and a similar expression occurs for $q_{2,1}$.

Thus the net exchange of power per unit area is:

$$q = \frac{\varepsilon_1\varepsilon_2}{(1-(1-\varepsilon_1)(1-\varepsilon_2))}.\sigma.(\theta_1{}^4-\theta_2{}^4) \text{ watts}$$

Let the emitter power per unit area be E and its temperature T_1, T_2 will be associated with the paint surface area and its surface is assumed 'grey' so that $\varepsilon_2 = \alpha$.

Using Weins displacement law for the emitter

$$T_1 = \frac{2897\,\mu\text{mK}}{2.63\,\mu\text{m}}$$

$$T_1 = 1101.5\,\text{K}$$

Again
$$E = \frac{\varepsilon_1.\varepsilon_2.\sigma.(T_1{}^4-T_2{}^4)}{[1-(1-\varepsilon_1).(1-\varepsilon_2)]}$$

Rearranging:

$$E - E.(1-\varepsilon_1).(1-\varepsilon_2) = \varepsilon_1.\varepsilon_2.\sigma.(T_1{}^4-T_2{}^4)$$

$$\therefore \quad E - E.(1-\varepsilon_2) + E.\varepsilon_1(1-\varepsilon_2) = \varepsilon_1.\varepsilon_2.\sigma.(T_1{}^4-T_2{}^4)$$

and
$$E.\varepsilon_2 = \varepsilon_1.\varepsilon_2.\sigma.(T_1{}^4-T_2{}^4) - E.\varepsilon_1.(1-\varepsilon_2)$$

Then
$$\varepsilon_1 = \frac{E\varepsilon_2}{[\varepsilon_2.\sigma.(T_1{}^4-T_2{}^4) - E(1-\varepsilon_2)]}$$

$$= \frac{36 \times 10^{-3} \times 0.6}{[0.6 \times 5.669 \times 10^{-8} \times (1101.5^4 - 293^4) - 0.4 \times 36 \times 10^{-3}]}$$

Giving
$$\varepsilon_1 = 0.609$$

IRH3

Discuss the frequency (wavelength) power density distribution for a black body heated successively to a range of temperatures. The relationship $\lambda_{max}.T = 2.9 \times 10^{-3}\,\text{mK}$ relates the wavelength (λ_{max}) at which maximum flux is emitted with the absolute temperature of a black body. How does this relate to the frequency–power distribution? Why is an incandescent lamp likely to be a more efficient source of heat than light?

Discuss emissivity and grey body radiation.

A 1 kW electric fire bar is designed to work at a temperature of

875 °C. Calculate the radiant efficiency of the bar. It may be
assumed that the fire bar has effective dimensions of 0.35 m long
and 8 mm diameter with an emissivity of 0.92. Determine its true
temperature if its effective brightness (black-body) temperature is
measured as 850 °C. Take the Stefan-Boltzmann constant $= 56.7$
$\times 10^{-12}$ kW/m^{2}K^4.

(Electroheat Tutorial — the author)

Solution

The distribution of radiative flux versus frequency is of the same
shape for every temperature. As the temperature increases the
height of the curve increases and the wavelength shortens as the
diagram shows for two temperatures T_1 and T_2 where $T_2 > T_1$.

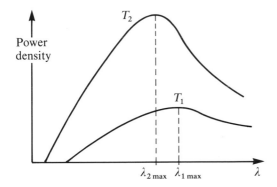

Noting the relationship

$$\lambda_{max} \cdot T = 2.9 \times 10^{-3} \, \text{mK}$$

this simply states that
knowing T_1 and T_2, $\lambda_{1_{max}}$
and $\lambda_{2_{max}}$ can be
determined.

Radiation flux is proportional to T^4 (T is the absolute temperature
of a body). A lamp depends on having sufficient of its radiation
characteristic in the visible (short) wavelength range (0.38–0.76 μm).
If the temperature is such that most of the emission lies outside the
visible range then it will be a more efficient source of heat than
light. Tungsten lamps operate at around 2500 °C and this will
produce an illumination efficiency of only 10%.

Emission of radiated heat from a 'real' surface is defined by the
term emissivity where

$$\varepsilon = \frac{E}{E_b}$$

E is the radiation flux from the surface (or body).

E_b is the flux from a black body at the same temperature.

The radiative energy emitted by the bar, Q, is given by

$Q =$ emissivity $\times$ black body radiation $\times$ area

$\quad = 0.92 \times 56.7 \times 10^{-12} \times (875 + 273)^4 \times 0.35 \times \pi \times 0.008$

$\quad = 0.8$ kW and a radiant efficiency of 80%.

If the effective brightness is measured as 850 °C then

black body radiation = emissivity × actual 'true' radiation

ie $T_b{}^4 = 0.92 \times T^4$ (the Stefan-Boltzmann constant cancels out)

$$\therefore \quad T = \frac{T_b}{(0.92)^{1/4}}$$

$$= \frac{(850 + 273)}{(0.92)^{1/4}}$$

$$= 873.7°C \text{ the 'true temperature'.}$$

IRH4

i) Given that the monochromatic power density is given by Planck's equation:

$$E_\lambda = \frac{2\pi hc^2}{\lambda^5 [e^{hc/\lambda KT}] - 1} \, \text{W/m}^3$$

Determine what constants make up Stefan Boltzmann's constant σ in the equation:

$$E = \sigma T^4 \, \text{W/m}^2$$

Where E = Total emissive power (W/m^2)

T = Body temperature (K).

ii) A material has a transmissivity characteristic which is a function of electromagnetic radiation as shown below:

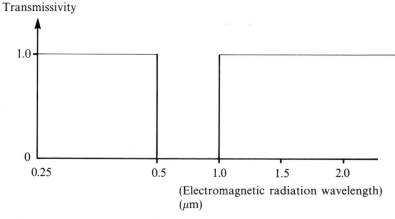

Transmissivity

It is proposed to heat this material with an IR emitter at a constant rate of 9.5 MJ for 30 seconds. The IR emitter operates at a temperature of 2200°C. If the emissivity of the emitter is 1 and the absorptivity of the material is 1 when its transmissivity is 0, calculate the area of the heater, given Wien's displacement relationship $\lambda . T = 2897 \, \mu$m.

iii) Was the choice of IR emitter correct, or would another be more appropriate? If so, state which type and why.

Note: Boltzmann's constant $(K) = 1.38 \times 10^{-23}\,\text{JK}^{-1}$

Planck constant $(h) = 6.62 \times 10^{-34}\,\text{J.sec.}$

Velocity of light $(c) = 3 \times 10^{8}\,\text{m/sec.}$

(Courtesy of University of Aston)

Solution

Part (i)

$$E_\lambda = \frac{2\pi hc^2}{\lambda^5 [e^{hc/\lambda KT} - 1]}\ \text{W/m}^3$$

where:

$T =$ Body Temp. (K)

$K =$ Boltzmann's const. $(1.38 \times 10^{-23}\,\text{JK}^{-1})$

$\lambda =$ Electromagnetic radiation wavelength (m)

$h =$ Planck constant $(6.62 \times 10^{-34}\,\text{J.sec.})$

$c =$ Velocity of light $(3 \times 10^{8}\,\text{m/s})$

$$E = \int_{\lambda=0}^{\infty} E_\lambda\, d\lambda$$

$$= \int_{0}^{\infty} \frac{2\pi hc^2}{\lambda^5}\left(\frac{1}{e^{\frac{hc}{\lambda KT}} - 1}\right) d\lambda \qquad (1)$$

Let

$$y = \frac{hc}{KT\lambda}$$

$$\therefore\quad \frac{dy}{d\lambda} = \frac{-hc}{KT}\cdot\left[\frac{1}{\lambda^2}\right]$$

Thus substitution into (1) gives:

$$E = -\int_{\infty}^{0} \frac{2\pi hc^2}{\left[\dfrac{hc}{\sigma.T}\right]^5}\cdot\frac{y^5}{y^2}\cdot\left[\frac{\sigma T}{hc}\right]\cdot\lambda^2\cdot\left[\frac{hc}{\sigma T}\right]^2\cdot\frac{1}{(e^y - 1)}\cdot dy$$

$$= \frac{2\pi hc^2}{\left[\dfrac{hc}{KT}\right]^4}\int_{0}^{\infty} \frac{y^3}{(e^y - 1)}\, dy$$

$$= \frac{2\pi K^4 T^4}{h^3 C^2}\left[\frac{\pi^4}{15}\right]$$

$$= \left[\frac{2\pi^5 K^4}{15 h^3 C^2}\right]\cdot T^4$$

but $E = \sigma T^4\ \text{W/m}^2$ as given, and thus:

$$\sigma = \left[\frac{2\pi K^4}{15h^3c^2}\right] = 5.67 \times 10^{-8} (\text{J/m}^2.\text{sK}) \text{ the Stefan-Boltzmann constant}$$

where the constants have been defined above.

Part (ii)

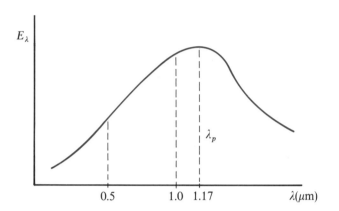

$$\lambda_p = \frac{2897}{T} \, \mu\text{mK}$$

$$\therefore \quad \lambda_p = \frac{2897}{2473}$$

$$\lambda_p = 1.17 \, \mu\text{m}$$

At $0.5 \, \mu\text{m}$

$$E_\lambda = \frac{2\pi \times 6.62 \times 10^{-34} \times (3 \times 10^8)^2}{(0.5 \times 10^{-6})^5 \times (e^z - 1)}$$

where

$$z = \frac{6.62 \times 10^{-34} \times 3 \times 10^8}{0.5 \times 10^{-6} \times 1.38 \times 10^{-23} \times 2473.0}$$

$$\therefore \quad E_\lambda = 1.06 \times 10^{11} \text{ W/m}^3$$

At $1 \, \mu\text{m}$

$$E_\lambda = \frac{2\pi \times 6.62 \times 10^{-34} \times (3 \times 10^8)^2}{(1 \times 10^{-6})^5 (e^{z'} - 1)}$$

where

$$z' = \frac{6.62 \times 10^{-34} \times 3 \times 10^8}{1.0 \times 10^{-6} \times 1.38 \times 10^{-23} \times 2473.0}$$

and

$$E_\lambda = 1.11 \times 10^{12} \text{ W/m}^3$$

$E \doteqdot$ Area under E_λ vs. λ curve.

$$= \left[\frac{1.11 \times 10^{12} + 1.06 \times 10^{11}}{2}\right] \times 0.5$$

$$E \doteqdot 0.304 \, \text{MW/m}^2$$

Required to heat at 9.5 MJ for 30 seconds

$$\therefore \quad \text{Power in} = \frac{9.5}{30} \, \text{M.J.s}^{-1}$$

$$\text{Power in} = 0.317 \, \text{MW}.$$

$\therefore$ Area of IR emitter

$$A = \frac{\text{Power absorbed (MW)}}{\text{Emissive power (MWm}^{-2})}$$

$$= \frac{0.317}{0.304}$$

$$A = 1.04 \, \text{m}^2$$

Part (iii)

Since the peak value of λ is not within the band where the material transmissivity is 0, then most of the electromagnetic energy is merely being transmitted through the material.

A better emitter would be one where λ_p occurred at say, 0.75 m, with an emitting temperature given by:

$$\therefore \quad T = \frac{2897}{0.75}$$

$$T = 3863 \, \text{K}$$

$$T = 3590 \, ^{\circ}\text{C}$$

IRH5

Using Planck's equation for the monochromatic power density prove Stefan-Boltzmann's equation.

What do you understand by the term 'grey body'. Give a simple example to show that the monochromatic absorptivity and emissivity of a grey body are equal. Discuss any assumptions made. Why is it necessary to introduce the notion of an average absorption coefficient?

An infra-red emitter with an operating temperature of 950 °C is to be used to stove paint. The paint has an absorptivity coefficient (α) of 1 for the infra-red energy between the wavelengths 2–4 μm. Outside this range it has a transmissivity coefficient (τ) of 1. To stove the paint requires the application of 12 MJ in 2 minutes. Calculate the surface area of the emitter and the kWh of electricity used by the unit.

Take Planck's equation as:

$$E_\lambda = \frac{2\pi h c^2}{\lambda^5 [e^{hc/KT} - 1]} \, \text{W/m}^3$$

where T is the absolute temperature in K

K is the Boltzmann's constant $(1.38 \times 10^{-23} \, \text{JK}^{-1})$

λ is the wavelength in metres

h is the Planck constant $(6.62 \times 10^{-34} \, \text{J sec.})$

c is the velocity of light $(3 \times 10^8 \, \text{ms}^{-1})$

Assume the IR emitter is a black body and that the total heat transfer is via RADIATION ONLY! You may use a straight line approximation between the three known points on the monochromatic emissive power density graph. Take Wein's displacement law as:

$$\lambda_{max} \, T = 289T \, \mu\text{mK}$$

(*University of Aston Electroheat Tutorial*)

Solution

The first part follows a similar pattern to the previous example IRH4 (i). The second part infers a knowledge of the $E - \lambda$-plot and the definition of monochromatic emissivity. Assumptions looked for are for the grey body to have uniform reflective and emissive properties over its surface which will be diffuse and even in temperature. Its transmittance should also be zero. The concept of average absorption coefficient is introduced as a *total* property of the material and to take notice of the variability of absorption with temperature and wavelength variations for real materials. Note that example IRH2 provides a convenient proof for the case of the parallel plates inferentially and for the mathematically inclined.

Using Wein's displacement law:

$$\lambda_{max} \, T = 2897 \, \mu\text{mK}$$

$$\therefore \quad \lambda_{max} = \frac{2897}{(950 + 273)}$$

$$\lambda_{max} = 2.37 \, \mu\text{m}$$

Using the Planck equation:

$$E_\lambda = \frac{2\pi h c^2}{\lambda^5 \cdot \left[e^{\frac{hc}{\lambda KT}} - 1 \right]}$$

Then

i) $E_{\lambda_1} = 3.27 \times 10^{10} \, \text{W.m}^{-3}$ from $T = 1223 \, \text{K}$, $\lambda = 2 \, \mu\text{m}$

ii) $E_{\lambda_{max}} = 3.52 \times 10^{10} \, \text{W.m}^3$ from $T = 1223 \, \text{K}$, $\lambda = 2.37 \, \mu\text{m}$

iii) $E_{\lambda_2} = 2.03 \times 10^{10}$ W.m^{-3} from $T = 1223$ K, $\lambda = 4\,\mu$m

and the area under the $E - \lambda$ graph $= 57.8$ kWm^{-2}.

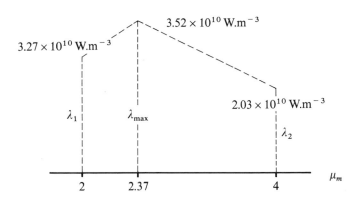

$$\text{Power required} = \frac{12}{2 \times 60} \text{ MJs}^{-1}$$

$$= 100 \text{ kW}$$

$$\text{Area of emitter} = \frac{100}{57.8}$$

$$= 1.73 \text{ m}^2$$

The total power required by the emitter is given by the Stefan-Boltzmann equation, i.e.:

$$\text{Total power} = \sigma A T^4$$

$$= 5.67 \times 10^{-8} \times 1.73 \times 1223^4 \text{ watts}$$

$$\text{Total power} = 219.5 \text{ kW}$$

This is required in 2 minutes so that the kWh used by the unit over 2 minutes

$$= 219.5 \times \frac{2}{60}$$

$$= 7.3 \text{ kWh}$$

IRH6

Describe any tests you would carry out on an industrial immersion heater both at the time of installation and commissioning and on a regular maintenance basis.

Immersion heaters with a total input of 5 kW are required using mineral insulated heated elements having a diameter of 3 mm and a resistance of 1 Ω/m at the operating temperature.

If the supply voltage is 240 V, determine the length of the heating element and the number of heaters required if the maximum power density of the element is 40 kW/m^2. What should be the diameter of the sheath, if the required length of the immersion heater is 1.2 m and the surface power density on the sheath is not to exceed 25 kW/m^2?

(Courtesy P. Tsappi (NELP)
Electroheat Teaching Workshops
British National Committee of
Electroheat 1979–1985)

Solution

The student should separate metal sheathed from non-metallic sheathed heaters and should identify the separate earthing requirements arising. He should then identify an acceptance test or performance, a cold insulation test and a high voltage flash test. The better student would mention briefly residual current devices (RCD) and a typical setting arrangement, e.g. 30 mA – 30 m.sec. (see reference 29).

$$\text{the minimum length of element} = \frac{\text{Power input}}{\text{Power density} \times \text{circumference}}$$

$$= \frac{5 \times 10^3}{40 \times 10^3 \times \pi \times 3 \times 10^{-3}}$$

$$= 13.25 \, \text{m}$$

The resistance for a power input of 5 kW

$$= \frac{V^2}{\text{Power}} = \frac{240^2}{5000}$$

$$= 11.52 \, \Omega$$

If only one element is used then

$$\left[\frac{1 \, \Omega}{\text{m}}\right] \times \text{length} = 11.52 \text{ which gives a length less than the}$$

required minimum length of 13.25 m.

If two elements are used each of 2.5 kW rating connected in parallel then each element will be 23.04 m long.

If d is the sheath diameter its surface area $= \pi \times d \times 1.2 \, \text{m}^2$.

The power density when both heaters are wound within one sheath

$$= \frac{5.0}{\pi \times d \times 1.2} = 25 \, \text{kW/m}^2$$

$$d = \frac{5.0 \times 10^3}{25 \times \pi \times 1.2} = 53 \, \text{mm}$$

Hence use two heating elements in parallel each 23 m long spirally wound to form one sheathed heater of diameter 53 mm or alternatively (and simultaneously reducing power density), two separately sheathed elements wired in parallel as one heater.

IRH7

An immersion heater is placed in a tank of water. If P is the rating of the heater, k is the power loss per each degree Celsius of temperature rise of the water, discuss the limitations of the equation $P = k.\theta_F$ in defining the rating of the heater where θ_F is the steady state temperature of the water.

A 10 kW immersion heater is available to heat a tank containing 105 litres of water to a temperature of 30 °C above ambient. The heat transfer coefficient of the tank surface is 15 W/m²°C and the surface area of the tank is 1.7 m². Calculate the time required for the water to reach the required temperature with the above immersion heater. How long will it take if the 10 kW heater is replaced by a 1 kW heater. Take the specific heat of water as 4.19 kJ/kg°C.

(Courtesy P. Tsappi (NELP)
Electroheat Teaching Workshops
British National Committee of
Electroheat 1979–1985)

Solution

In maintaining or raising process temperatures and in melting applications, the required installed power will have to be provided to meet a given specification. This can be calculated by equating the energy supplied to the sum of the energy used in raising the temperature of the product and the energy lost by convection, conduction and radiation.

$$Pdt = Smd\theta + k\theta dt \tag{1}$$

where P is the required power in W

$dt =$ time interval for the temperature to raise by $d\theta$ °C

$S =$ specific heat of the material being heated in J/kgK and can be temperature dependent

$m =$ mass of the material in kg

$k =$ power loss per each degree temperature rise in W/°C.

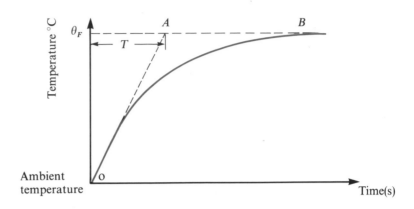

Equation (1) is a differential equation with a solution of the form

$$\theta = \theta_F(1 - e^{-t/T}) \tag{2}$$

where θ_F is the final temperature and therefore the temperature/ time graph is an exponential curve of the form shown. The constant T is referred to as the thermal time constant since it has the units of time and can be related to S, m and k as follows:

rewriting equation (1) as

$$P = \frac{Smd\theta}{dt} + k\theta$$

in the steady state $P = k\theta_F$ and if there were no losses, the final temperature would be reached in time $T(s)$.

i.e.
$$P = Sm\frac{\theta_F}{T} = \frac{SmP}{Tk}$$

or
$$T = \frac{Sm}{k}(s)$$

During the heating up period, the temperature rise follows curve OB, but for calculating the power to be supplied it can be assumed that the temperature rise follows OA provided:

a)   the heating up time is short compared to T

or b)   the power available is sufficiently large for the process temperature to be on the linear part of the temperature/time curve.

Under these conditions the energy losses during the heating up period can be averaged. The energy losses can be calculated by the application of heat transfer formulae or available graphs can be used provided the conditions for which the data referred to are known and match the case in hand. In using thermal conductivity values for insulation, it should be noted that it is temperature dependent and manufacturers' data should therefore be consulted.

50

Taking
$$P = k\theta_F$$
$$10,000 = 15 \times 1.7 \times \theta_F = 25.5 \times \theta_F$$

or
$$\theta_F = 392\,°C$$

The time constant $T = \dfrac{4190 \times 105}{15 \times 1.7 \times 3600} = 4.79$ hrs.

From equation (2)

$30 = 392(1 - e^{-t_1/T})$ or $t_1 = 22.9$ min. where t_1 is the heating up time.

Using equation (1) instead with $d\theta = 30\,°C$,

$$10,000 = 4190 \times 105 \times \frac{30}{t} + \frac{25.5 \times 30}{2}$$

or $t = 22.87$ min., i.e. the same answer as when using the exponential solution. The reason for this is of course that $T \gg t$.

Resolving for the 1 kW heater, the new time t_2 is given by:

$$1000 = 25.5\theta_F \qquad \theta_F = 39\,°C$$

$$30 = 39(1 - e^{-t_2/287}) \text{ or } t_2 = 420 \text{ min.}$$

[*NOTE:* The solution using equation (1) gives $t_2 = 356$ min. which does not agree with the correct answer of 420 min.]

IRH8

Show that the following formula can be used to determine the wire diameter for a heating element.

$$d = \sqrt[3]{\frac{4P\rho 10^9}{P\pi^2 R_H}} = \frac{1}{6.27} \cdot \sqrt[3]{\frac{(P)^2}{(V)^2 p}} \cdot 10^{11}$$

and that the units of

$$\frac{P}{p} \cdot \frac{C_T}{R_H} \text{ are } m^2/\Omega$$

where
$\quad d =$ wire diameter in mm

$\quad P =$ element rating in W

$\quad \rho =$ resistivity in Ωm

$\quad p =$ admissible surface loading W/m²

$\quad R_H =$ resistance of element hot Ω

$\quad R_C =$ resistance of element at 20 °C Ω

$\quad V =$ supply voltage V

$\quad C_T =$ ratio of $\dfrac{R_H}{R_C}$.

Select the diameter of wire and its length for the construction of a 1 kW at 240 V spiral element. The estimated operating temperature of the element is 800 °C and the recommended surface load is 40 kW/m². If the element is not to exceed 1.3 m in length, propose a suitable number of turns and spiral diameter. The ratio of pitch to wire diameter can be taken as 2, and the manufacturers' data for Nikrothal 80 should be used.

Calculate the temperature of the element in the steady state if the element is suspended horizontally in still air at 20 °C. The emissivity of the element material can be assumed constant at 0.9. The heat transfer coefficient can be assumed to be given approximately by $1.32 \left[\dfrac{d\theta}{d} \right]^{1/4}$ W/m²°C where $\Delta\theta$ is the temperature above ambient and d the wire diameter. Stefan Boltzmann constant $\sigma = 5.67 \times 10^{-8}$ W/m² K⁴.

(Courtesy P. Tsappi (NELP) Electroheat Teaching Workshops British National Committee of Electroheat 1979–1985)

Solution

$$P = \frac{V^2}{R_H} = \frac{V^2 \pi d^2}{4\rho l}$$

or

$$d^2 = \frac{p 4\rho l}{PR_H \dfrac{A_s \pi}{A_s}} = \frac{P4\rho}{R_H \rho \pi^2 d} \qquad (1)$$

when $A_1 =$ surface area $= \pi.d.l$

From (1)

$$d = \sqrt[3]{\frac{4.P.\rho.10^9}{p.\pi^2.R_H}} \quad \text{since } R_H = \frac{V}{I}$$

$$d = \frac{1}{6.27} \sqrt[3]{\left(\frac{P}{V}\right)^2 \frac{P}{p} 10^{11}} \qquad \text{QED}$$

Again

$$P = I^2 R_H = I^2 R_c C_T$$

or

$$\frac{P}{A_s} = p = \frac{I^2 R_c C_T}{A_s} = \frac{P}{R_H} \frac{R_c C_T}{A_s}$$

and

$$\frac{P}{p} \frac{C_T}{R_H} = \frac{A_s}{R_c} = \frac{m^2}{\Omega} \qquad \text{QED}$$

Diameter mm	Resistance per length unit Ω/m 20°C	cm²/Ω 20°C	Weight per length unit g/m	Surface per length unit cm²/m	Cross sectional area mm²	Diameter mm
0.95	1.54	19.4	5.88	29.9	0.708	0.95
0.90	1.71	16.5	5.28	28.3	0.636	0.90
0.85	1.92	13.9	4.71	26.7	0.567	0.85
0.80	2.17	11.6	4.17	25.1	0.502	0.80
0.75	2.47	9.55	3.67	23.6	0.442	0.75
0.70	2.83	7.76	3.19	22.0	0.385	0.70
0.65	3.29	6.22	2.75	20.4	0.332	0.65
0.60	3.86	4.89	2.35	18.9	0.283	0.60
0.55	4.59	3.77	1.97	17.3	0.237	0.55
0.50	5.55	2.83	1.63	15.7	0.196	0.50
0.48	6.03	2.50	1.50	15.1	0.181	0.48
0.45	6.85	2.06	1.32	14.1	0.159	0.45
0.42	7.87	1.68	1.15	13.2	0.138	0.42
0.40	8.67	1.45	1.04	12.6	0.126	0.40
0.38	9.62	1.24	0.938	11.9	0.113	0.38
0.35	11.3	0.971	0.799	11.0	0.0962	0.35
0.32	13.6	0.735	0.667	10.0	0.0804	0.32
0.30	15.4	0.611	0.587	9.43	0.0707	0.30
0.28	17.7	0.497	0.511	8.80	0.0615	0.28
0.26	20.5	0.398	0.441	8.16	0.0531	0.26
0.25	22.2	0.354	0.407	7.85	0.0491	0.25
0.24	24.1	0.313	0.375	7.54	0.0452	0.24
0.23	26.3	0.275	0.344	7.22	0.0415	0.23
0.22	28.7	0.241	0.315	6.91	0.0380	0.22
0.21	31.5	0.209	0.287	6.59	0.0346	0.21
0.20	34.7	0.181	0.261	6.28	0.0314	0.20
0.19	38.4	0.155	0.235	5.97	0.0283	0.19
0.18	42.8	0.132	0.211	5.66	0.0254	0.18
0.17	48.0	0.111	0.188	5.34	0.0227	0.17
0.16	54.2	0.0927	0.167	5.03	0.0201	0.16
0.15	61.7	0.0764	0.147	4.71	0.0177	0.15
0.14	70.8	0.0621	0.128	4.40	0.0154	0.14
0.13	82.1	0.0497	0.110	4.08	0.0133	0.13
0.12	96.4	0.0391	0.0939	3.77	0.0113	0.12
0.11	115	0.0301	0.0789	3.46	0.00950	0.11
0.10	139	0.0226	0.0652	3.14	0.00785	0.10
0.09	171	0.0165	0.0528	2.83	0.00636	0.09
0.08	217	0.0116	0.0417	2.51	0.00502	0.08
0.07	283	0.00776	0.0319	2.20	0.00385	0.07
0.06	386	0.00489	0.0235	1.89	0.00283	0.06
0.05	555	0.00283	0.0163	1.57	0.00196	0.05
0.04	867	0.00145	0.0104	1.26	0.00126	0.04
0.03	1542	0.000611	0.00587	0.943	0.000707	0.03

To obtain resistivity at working temperature multiply by the factor C_t in the following table:

°C	20	100	200	300	400	500	600	700	800	900	1000	1100	1200	1300	1400
C_t	1.00	1.01	1.02	1.03	1.04	1.05	1.04	1.04	1.04	1.04	1.05	1.06	1.07		

Table. *Heating element data Nikrothal 80 (Courtesy Boulton Kanthal AB)*

$$R_H = \frac{V^2}{p} = \frac{240^2}{1000} = 57.6\,\Omega$$

at 800 °C, $C_T = 1.04$ for Nikrothal 80

surface power density $= 40\ kW/m^3 = 4.0\ W/cm^2$

$$\frac{P.C_T}{p.R_H} = \frac{1000 \times 1.04}{4 \times 57.6} = 4.5 \left[\frac{cm^2}{\Omega}\right]$$

From the table, the nearest value is 4.89 with a wire diameter of 0.6 mm.

The operating power density will be $\dfrac{1000 \times 1.04}{4.89 \times 57.6} = 3.7\ W\ cm^{-2}$

The resistance at 20 °C $= \dfrac{R_H}{C_T} = \dfrac{57.6}{1.04} = 55.38\,\Omega$

from the table $\Omega m^{-1} = 3.86$

hence $l = \dfrac{55.38}{3.86} = 14.3$ (or 14,300 mm).

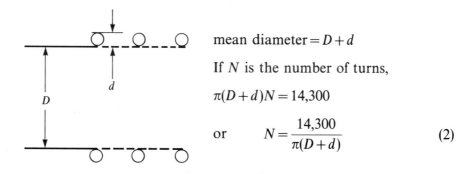

mean diameter $= D + d$

If N is the number of turns,

$$\pi(D+d)N = 14{,}300$$

or $\qquad N = \dfrac{14{,}300}{\pi(D+d)}$ (2)

Length of spiral $= N \times 2d = 1700$

thus from (2)

$$\frac{14{,}300}{\pi(D+d)} \times 2d = 1300 \tag{3}$$

with $d = 0.6$ mm (see above)

then $D = 3.6$ mm from (3).

Then $N = \dfrac{14{,}300}{\pi(3.6+0.6)} = 1084$ turns

In the steady state,

$$\frac{\text{Power input}}{\text{Unit surface}} = \frac{\text{Power loss}}{\text{Unit surface}}$$

As before the operating power density remains at 3.7 W/cm².

$$\therefore \quad 3.7 = \frac{0.9 \times 5.67 \times 10^{-8}}{10^4}[(T+273)^4 - (20+273)^4]$$
$$+ \frac{1.32}{10^4}\left(\frac{T-20}{0.006}\right)^{1/4}.(T-20)$$

solving for T,

$$T = 500\,°C \text{ will be found as a solution.}$$

IRH9

5 kg of polypropylene granules are to be heated to 250 °C in a press each hour. The steel plattens weigh 102 kg each and measure 0.6 m long, 0.3 m wide, 75 mm thick and must be preheated to 250 °C in half an hour. The plattens are not insulated.

The heating process is carried out with the plattens closed at an ambient temperature of 20 °C. The heat losses during opening and closing the plattens may be ignored.

The steel has a specific heat of 0.46 kJ/kg and an emissivity of 0.8. The density of polypropylene is 900 kg/m^3 and its mean specific heat is 533 J/kg.K. The surface to surface heat transfer coefficient is 1.8 J/m^{2}K$^{1.25}$. The Stefan-Boltzmann constant is 5.67×10^{-8}.Wm^{-2}K^{-4}.

What is the installed power required?

(Modified by the author from references 3 and 22)

Solution
The heat required to increase the temperature of the polypropylene is:
$$Q_p = m.C_{pp}.(\theta - \theta_{ambient})$$
$$= 5 \times 533 \times 230$$
$$= 613.kJ$$

The heat required to raise the steel plattens to 250 °C is:
$$Q_s = 2 \times 102 \times 0.46 \times 230$$
$$= 21.6\,kJ$$

Effective exposed area of the steel plattens is:
$$A_s = 2.[(0.6 \times 0.3) + 0.075(1.2 + 0.6)]$$
$$= 0.63\,m^2$$

The heat losses from the plattens at 250 °C are:
$$Q_T = 1.8 \times 0.63 \times [230]^{5/4} + 0.8 \times 5.67 \times 10^{-8} \times 0.63 \times [523^4 - 293^4]$$
$$\doteqdot 3\,kW$$

Thus the heating up loss may be taken as $\dfrac{Q_T}{2}$ say 1.5 kW, and the power to heat up the plattens in the *first* half an hour is

$$P_1 = \frac{21.6 \times 10^3}{3600} \times 2 + 1.5 = 13.5 \, \text{kW}$$

The heat required to heat 5 kg of polypropylene granules each hour is:

$$P_2 = \frac{613}{3600}$$

$$= 0.17 \, \text{kW}$$

Thus the running loss is about 3.17 kW.

Therefore install 13.5 kW which will meet both starting up and running conditions.

IRH10

(a) Discuss briefly safety aspects associated with the use of surface heating tapes in a hazardous environment.

(b) A 50 mm internal diameter, 50 m long steel pipe, insulated by 20 mm of glass fibre, is to be maintained at a temperature of 35 °C with a possible ambient of −5 °C.

A heating tape, having a linear loading of 12 W/m and capable of compensating for the heat losses from the pipe, is to be designed and constructed from 0.6 mm diameter copper wire having an average temperature coefficient of resistance of 0.004/°C and a resistivity of $1.3 \times 10^{-8} \, \Omega \text{m}$.

The thermal "resistance" of the material between the heating element of the tape and the pipe wall is 2 °C m/W. For the 240 V single-phase supply:

i) calculate the length of the wire for the heating element,

ii) explain, making any necessary calculations, how the length of wire will be accommodated within the tape,

iii) with an ambient temperature of 6 °C calculate the element temperature under normal operating conditions and the starting current.

Losses from pipes are given in table IRH10.

(*Courtesy of NELP (B.Sc. Finals, 1981)*)

Solution

(a) References 28, 33, 34 and 35 provide a useful background.

(b) Pipe to ambient temperature $= 35 - (-5) = 40 \, °\text{C}$

Table *IRH10*

Basic heat loss [W/m]

$\dfrac{\Delta T}{[°C]}$

Pipe size (internal) Inch		$\frac{1}{2}$	$\frac{3}{4}$	1	$1\frac{1}{4}$	$1\frac{1}{2}$	2	$2\frac{1}{2}$	3	4	6	8	10	12	14	16	18	20	24
mm		15	20	25	32	40	50	65	80	100	150	200	250	300	350	400	450	500	600
Insulation Thickness 10 mm	20	7.2	8.4	10	12	13.4	16.2	19	23	29	41	52	64	74	81	92	103	115	137
	30	10.7	12.6	15	18	20.2	24.4	29	34	43	61	78	95	111	121	138	155	172	205
	40	14.3	16.8	20	24	26.8	32.5	38	45	57	81	104	127	148	162	184	207	229	274
	60	21.5	25.2	30	36	40.2	48.7	58	68	86	122	156	191	222	243	276	310	343	411
	80	28.6	33.7	40	48.1	53.6	65	77	90	114	163	208	255	295	323	368	413	458	548
	100	36	42.4	50.3	60.5	67.4	81.7	97	114	144	205	261	320	372	407	463	520	576	699
	120	44.5	52.3	62.2	74.8	83.4	101	119	140	177	253	322	395	459	502	572	641	711	850
20 mm	20	4.6	5.0	6.1	7.2	7.9	9.4	11	13	16	22	29	34	40	44	50	56	61	73
	30	6.8	7.9	9.1	10.8	11.9	14.2	16	19	24	33	42	51	60	68	75	83	92	110
	40	9.1	10.6	12.2	14.4	15.8	18.8	22	25	32	44	56	68	80	88	99	111	123	147
	60	13.6	15.7	18.2	21.6	23.9	28.2	33	38	48	67	84	103	120	131	149	167	184	220
	80	18.2	21	24.4	28.8	31.8	37.7	44	51	63	89	113	137	160	175	199	222	246	293
	100	23	26.4	30.7	36.2	40	47.4	55	64	80	112	142	172	202	220	250	280	310	369
	120	28.4	32.8	37.9	44.9	49.4	58.7	68	79	99	138	175	212	249	272	309	346	383	456
30 mm	20	3.6	4.1	4.7	5.5	6	7	8	9	11	16	20	24	28	31	34	38	43	51
	30	5.4	6.1	7.1	8.2	9	10.6	12	14	17	24	30	36	42	46	52	58	64	76
	40	7.3	8.3	9.5	10.9	12	14	16	19	23	31	40	48	56	61	69	77	85	101
	60	10.9	12.4	14.2	16.4	18	21	24	28	34	47	59	72	84	91	103	116	128	152
	80	14.5	16.4	18.8	21.8	24	28	32	37	46	63	79	96	112	122	138	154	170	202
	100	18.2	20.8	23.8	27.6	30.1	35.3	41	47	57	79	100	121	141	153	174	194	214	254
	120	22.7	25.7	29.4	34.1	37.3	43.6	50	58	71	98	123	149	174	190	215	240	265	315
40 mm	20	3.1	3.5	4	4.6	4.9	5.8	7	8	9	12	16	19	22	24	27	29	33	39
	30	4.7	5.3	6	6.8	7.4	8.6	10	11	14	19	23	28	33	35	40	44	49	58
	40	6.2	7.1	7.9	9.1	10	11.5	13	15	18	25	31	37	43	47	53	59	66	78
	60	9.4	10.6	12	13.7	14.9	17.3	20	22	27	37	46	56	65	71	80	89	98	117
	80	12.5	14	16	18.2	19.9	23	26	30	37	50	62	75	87	94	107	110	131	155
	100	15.7	17.6	20	23	25.1	28.9	33	38	46	63	78	94	109	119	134	150	165	196
	120	19.6	22	24.8	28.4	31	35.9	41	47	57	72	96	116	135	147	166	185	204	242
50 mm	20	2.8	3.1	3.5	4	4.3	5	6	7	8	10	13	16	18	19	22	24	27	32
	30	4.2	4.7	5.3	6	6.5	7.4	9	10	12	16	19	23	27	29	33	37	40	48
	40	5.6	6.2	7.1	8	8.6	10	11	13	16	21	26	31	36	39	44	49	66	78
	60	8.4	9.4	10.6	12	13.8	15	17	19	23	31	39	46	54	58	66	73	80	95
	80	11.3	12.5	14	16.1	17.4	19.9	23	26	31	42	51	62	72	78	88	97	107	127
	100	14.2	15.7	17.8	20.2	21.8	25.1	28	32	39	52	65	78	90	98	110	123	135	160
	120	17.5	19.6	22	25	27	31.1	35	40	48	65	80	96	112	121	136	152	167	198

From table losses $= 18.8$ W/m

$\therefore$ total losses to be compensated $= 18.8 \times 50 = 940$ W*

$\therefore$ $940 = \dfrac{240^2}{R}$ or $R = 61.3\,\Omega$

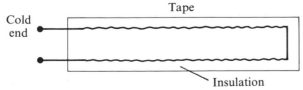

*Some solutions could include a contingency factor which would be acceptable.

$$R = \rho \frac{l}{a} = \frac{1.3 \times 10^{-8} l}{\pi (0.3 \times 10^{-3})^2} = 61.3 \quad \text{or} \quad l = 13.3 \times 10^2 \, \text{m}$$

If L is the length of tape $12 \times L = 940$ or $L = 78 \, \text{m}$

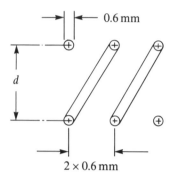

Length of wire per metre length of tape $= \dfrac{1330}{2 \times 78} = 8.52$

$(2 \times 78$ because go and return to be accommodated$)$

$$\text{Number of turns/metre} = \frac{1000}{2 \times 0.6} = 833$$

$$\therefore \quad d = \frac{8.52}{\pi \times 833} = 3.25 \, \text{mm}$$

The wire will be spiralled on a flexible glass fibre core and insulated in a PVC extension sheath. If T_e = temperature of element and T_p = temperature of pipe

then
$$T_e - T_p = 2 \times 12 \quad \text{or} \quad T_e = 35 + 24 = 59 \, ^\circ\text{C}$$

$$R = R_o(1 + \alpha_o t) \quad \text{or} \quad 61.3 = R_o(1 + 0.004 \times 59)$$

or
$$R_o = 49.5 \, \Omega$$

$$\therefore \quad I(\text{start}) = \frac{240}{49.5} = 4.85 \, \text{Amps}$$

IRH11

A plumbago ladle is designed to hold 50 kg of iron at 1400 °C. It is large enough to take an electric element cradle made of alumina bricks cemented together.

Calculations show that 7.5 kW will preheat the ladle to a temperature in excess of 800 °C in about four hours.

The cradle has dimensions 22 cm × 22 cm × 38 cm (high). Using wire of 16 mm diameter of resistance 0.558 Ω/metre use the cradle and design the element and its support. Assume a voltage supply of 240 V.

(Example also applicable to section on metal melting.)

(The author)

Solution

This is an important example showing how a simple element cradle can be used in a foundry ladle heating application. A cautionary note: care must be taken to ensure that exposed elements are protected from coming into contact with the metal casing of the ladle with power on. The student could be asked to comment on the use of a (safer) lower voltage.

Solution

$$\frac{V^2}{R} = 7.5 \times 10^3$$

$$R = \frac{240^2}{7.5 \times 10^3} = 7.7 \text{ ohms}$$

$$\text{Length of element} = \frac{7.7}{0.558} = 13.76 \text{ metres}$$

$$\text{Current} = \frac{240}{7.7} = 31 \text{ amps}$$

Hence fuse at 35 amps.

The student would then be expected to suggest a grooved *helix* in the refractory cradle to mount the element (suggest 17 grooves, of pitch 1.5 cm) each groove 60 mm deep, 30 mm wide. Total number of turns will be (approx.) 13.76/0.88, i.e. 16.

Students may wish to discuss termination.

CHAPTER 4

Induction heating

4.1. Background to the teaching

The fundamental problem with teaching this topic lies with the easiest practical form (a helical coil around a right circular cylinder workpiece) producing a complicated analysis which really requires the use of Bessel functions. Nicholls attempts to by-pass this difficulty[38] by quoting the skin effect equation and thereafter tackling the problem by consideration of a conduction toroid in the workpiece.

If induction heating is taught as part of a general course on electroheat or even where heating mechanisms over a significant part of the electromagnetic field frequency spectrum are considered serious thought to an introduction using a unified approach suggested by Metaxas[21] should be given (see Chapter 2).

It may well be, however, that induction heating will be taught either in isolation or perhaps in combination with direct resistance heating. In these cases Hammond[14] will be found particularly helpful with Davies and Simpson[20] probably providing the most recent analytical approaches relevant to the subject. Unfortunately Davies and Simpson quote by analogy the Bessel function approach to the heating of right circular cylinders and refer to earlier sources (e.g. 39 and 40) with all the complications of mixed units.

A practical view of the subject now unfortunately out of date by Lozinskii is, nevertheless, full of applications[41]. Limited background reading exists[6,12,42] and for those seeking a mathematical background Pipes and Harvill[43] provide a reasonable source.

If the early empirical approach is acceptable then Nicholls[38] provides a beginning and the first example IH1 relating to a copper coil, surrounding a cylindrical workpiece is a useful introduction to obtaining a feeling for the units and parameter sizes. IH2 continues this technique.

A logical approach is to start with the analysis first of a semi-infinite slab from which the skin effect and depth of penetration phenomena can be deduced. Realistically this calls for a knowledge of Maxwell's Laws from which the appropriate diffusion equation in current density, flux density and field intensity can be derived. It is an easy step to the slab heated from two sides and to thin workpieces. The geometric form of the resulting equations leads by analogy to the cylinder. Example IH3 starts this theme. It is now necessary to consider thermal aspects of the situation. The definitive work is by Carslaw and Jaeger[1]. It is however a difficult treatise. Davies and Simpson[20] merely quote relevant parts to derive the detail. However, much can be achieved in understanding the simple situations using surface power density and workpiece enthalpy (example IH4). The Teaching Note by Davies[44] provides a convenient lecture source.

Returning to the cylindrical workpiece, by now the student will have been reminded of the generalised transformer equation and will derive the transfer equation for the semi-infinite slab:

$$P = \frac{H_s^2}{2\sigma\delta}$$

P = power loss per unit area.

H_s = surface magnetic field strength.

σ = conductivity.

δ = penetration depth.

Manipulation of these factors is given in example IH5. A definitive treatment of the cylinder is not really a candidate for a worked example of an examination type without much simplification.

Finally, examples of a power supply linking to a workpiece (IH7 and IH11) are given which can be the source of much ingenuity.

The important striation phenomenon[41] is tested in examples IH6 and 10. Although empirical the examples stress the various limiting factors.

4.2. The worked examples

IH1

Data: Resistivity of steel between 20 and 850 °C,

$\rho_{20} = 0.2\,\mu\Omega\text{m}, \quad \alpha_{20} = 0.00572\,\text{K}^{-1}.$

Resistivity of steel between 850° and 1400°C,

$\rho_{850} = 1.15\,\mu\Omega\text{m}, \quad \alpha_{850} = 0.00021\,\text{K}^{-1}$

Resistivity of copper from 20° upwards,

$\rho_{20} = 0.017\,\mu\Omega\text{m}, \quad \alpha_{20} = 0.004\,\text{K}^{-1}.$

Relative permeability of steel,

$$\mu_r = 800$$

Permeability of free space,

$$\mu_o = 4\pi \times 10^{-7}$$

Specific heat capacity of water,

$$= 4.19 \, \text{kJ/kgK}$$

The above data apply to a cylindrical, steel workpiece enclosed in a copper coil. Carry out the following calculations, assuming a supply frequency of $f = 10 \, \text{kHz}$.

1. Determine the integrated resistivity, ρ_m, of steel for the range 20–750 °C and compare it with the spot values at 385° and 1200°.

2. Assuming that permeability is effectively reduced by a factor of 4:1 due to saturation, estimate the mean skin depth, δ_w, for the 20–750 °C temperature range and compare it with the spot value at 1200 °C.

3. Given that the workpiece is cylindrical, of diameter $D_w = 25 \, \text{mm}$ and length $L_w = 50 \, \text{mm}$, calculate the effective resistance, R_w, for the 20–750° temperature range assuming the current to be uniformly distributed over one skin depth.

4. If a superficial power density of $10 \, \text{MW/m}^2$ is required over the cylindrical surface determine the total power, P_w, and the current, I_w, needed in the workpiece.

5. Given that the coil has $N = 4$ turns, what current, I_c, should it carry?

6. Estimate the power, P_c, lost in the coil if its mean temperature is 50 °C, its overall length is $L_c = 50 \, \text{mm}$ and there are gaps of $g = 5 \, \text{mm}$ between successive turns and between the coil and the workpiece.

7. Hence determine the efficiency, η, of the coil. Compare this with a value obtained from consideration of resistivities and permeabilities alone.

8. Calculate the temperature rise, ΔT, of the cooling water through the coil if its flow rate is 5 litre/min, ignoring other mechanisms of heat transfer from and to the coil.

(From reference 38)

Solution

1. *Integrated resistivity*
Working in $\mu\Omega$m, ie omitting the factor of 10^{-6},

$$\rho_{20} = 0.2 \; \mu\Omega\text{m}$$

$$\rho_{750} = \rho_{20}(1 + \alpha_{20}(750 - 20))$$

$$= (0.2)(1 + (0.00572)(750 - 20)) = 1.035 \; \mu\Omega\text{m}$$

For 20–750° range:

$$\sqrt{\rho_m} = \tfrac{1}{2}(\sqrt{\rho_{20}} + \sqrt{\rho_{750}})$$

$$\rho_m = (\tfrac{1}{2}(\sqrt{0.2} + \sqrt{1.035}))^2 = 0.536 \; \mu\Omega\text{m}$$

$$\rho_{385} = (0.2)(1 + (0.00572)(385 - 20)) = 0.618 \; \mu\Omega\text{m}$$

$$\rho_{1200} = \rho_{850}(1 + \alpha_{850}(1200 - 850))$$

$$= (1.15)(1 + (0.00021)(1200 - 850)) = 1.235 \; \mu\Omega\text{m}$$

2. *Skin depth*

$$\delta = \sqrt{\frac{2\rho}{\mu_o \mu_r \omega}}, \text{ where } \omega = 2\pi f$$

For 20–750°C range:

$$\delta_w = \left[\frac{(2)(0.536 \times 10^{-6})}{(4\pi \times 10^{-7})(\frac{800}{4})(2\pi \times 10{,}000)} \right]^{1/2} = 0.261 \text{ mm}$$

At 1200°C:

$$\delta_w = \left[\frac{(2)(1.235 \times 10^{-6})}{(4\pi \times 10^{-7})(1)(2\pi \times 10{,}000)} \right]^{1/2} = 5.59 \text{ mm}$$

3. *Resistance of workpiece*

$$R_w = \frac{\rho_w \pi D_w}{\delta_w L_w}$$

$$= \frac{(0.536 \times 10^{-6})(\pi)(0.025)}{(0.261 \times 10^{-3})(0.050)} = 0.00323 \; \Omega$$

4. *Workpiece power and current*

$$P_w = (\text{power density}) \times (\text{surface area})$$

$$= (10 \times 10^6)(\pi \times 0.025 \times 0.050) = 39.27 \text{ kW}$$

$$P_w = I_w{}^2 R_w$$

$$I_w = \left(\frac{P_w}{R_w} \right)^{1/2}$$

$$= \sqrt{\frac{39{,}270}{0.00323}} = 3487 \text{ A}$$

5. Coil current

$$I_c = \frac{I_w}{N}$$

$$= \frac{(3487)}{(4)} = 872 \, A$$

6. Power loss in coil

Resistivity of copper at $50\,°C$:

$$\rho_c = \rho_{20}(1 + \alpha_{20}(50 - 20))$$

$$= (0.017 \times 10^{-6})(1 + (0.004)(50 - 20) = 0.0190 \, \mu\Omega m$$

Skin depth in copper:

$$\delta = \sqrt{\frac{2\rho}{\mu_o \mu_r \omega}}$$

$$\delta_c = \left(\frac{(2)(0.0190 \times 10^{-6})}{(4\pi \times 10^{-7})(1)(2\pi \times 10,000)}\right)^{1/2} = 0.696 \, mm$$

Cross-sectional area of current path:

$$A_p = \delta_c \left(\frac{L_c - (N-1)(0.005)}{N}\right)$$

$$= (0.696 \times 10^{-3})\left(\frac{(0.050) - (3)(0.005)}{(4)}\right) = 6.09 \times 10^{-6} \, m^2$$

Length of current path:

$$L_p = N\pi(D_w + 2g)$$

$$= (4)(\pi)((0.025) + (2 \times 0.005)) = 0.440 \, m$$

Resistance of coil:

$$R_c = \frac{\rho_c L_p}{A_p}$$

$$= \frac{(0.019 \times 10^{-6})(0.440)}{(6.09 \times 10^{-6})} = 0.00137 \, \Omega$$

Power loss:

$$P_c = I_c^2 R_c$$

$$= (872)^2(0.00137) = 1.04 \, kW$$

7. Efficiency

(a) $$\eta = \frac{P_w}{P_w + P_c} \times 100$$

$$= \frac{(39.27)}{(39.27) + (1.04)} \times (100) = 97.4\%$$

(b) $\eta = \dfrac{1}{1 + \sqrt{\dfrac{\rho_c \mu_c}{\rho_w \mu_w}}} \times 100$

$= \dfrac{1}{1 + \left[\dfrac{(0.019)(1)}{(0.536)(200)}\right]^{1/2}} \times (100) = 98.7\%$

8. *Water temperature rise*

$$\Delta T = \dfrac{P_c}{(\text{mass flow rate})(\text{specific heat capacity})}$$

$$= \dfrac{(1.04)}{(5 \div 60)(4.19)} = 2.98 \text{ K}$$

IH2

Determine the rates at which heat in kW is generated in a cylindrical steel workpiece and in an induction heating coil surrounding it. The workpiece is of length 50 mm, diameter 25 mm, resistivity 0.4 $\mu\Omega$m and relative permeability 200. The coil consists of 4 turns of 10 mm-square-section, copper tube and is 50 mm long, with inside diameter 30 mm and resistivity 0.02 $\mu\Omega$m, and carries a current of 500 A at a frequency of 450 kHz. State any assumptions which you make.

Given:

$$\text{skin depth } \delta = \sqrt{\dfrac{2\rho}{\mu_o \mu_r \omega}}; \quad \mu_o = 4\pi \times 10^{-7}$$

Describe in general terms how the induction heating of steel billets is affected by non-uniformity of resistivity and permeability and by heat losses.

(From reference 38)

Solution

For workpiece

$$\text{Skin depth } \delta_w = \sqrt{\dfrac{2\rho_w}{\mu_o \mu_r \omega}} = \left[\dfrac{(2)(0.4 \times 10^{-6})}{(4\pi \times 10^{-7})(200)(2\pi \times 450{,}000)}\right]^{1/2}$$

$$= 0.0335 \text{ mm, assuming uniform } \rho \text{ and } \mu$$

$$\text{Resistance } R_w = \dfrac{\rho \pi d_w}{\delta_w l_w} = \dfrac{(0.4 \times 10^{-6})(\pi)(0.025)}{(0.0335 \times 10^{-3})(0.05)}$$

$$= 0.0188 \,\Omega, \text{ assuming current confined to one skin depth}$$

$$\text{Current } I_w = N I_c = (4)(500) = 2000 \text{ A}$$

$$\text{Power } P_w = I_w^2 R_w = (2000)^2 (0.0188) = 75.2 \text{ kW}$$

For coil

$$\text{Skin depth } \delta_c = \sqrt{\frac{2\rho_c}{\mu_o\omega}} = \left[\frac{2(0.02 \times 10^{-6})}{(4\pi \times 10^{-7})(2\pi \times 450{,}000)}\right]^{1/2}$$

$$= 0.106 \text{ mm, assuming uniform } \rho$$

$$\text{Resistance } R_c = \frac{N\rho_c d_c}{\delta_c t_c} \text{ where } t_c = \text{width of tube}$$

$$= \frac{(4)(0.02 \times 10^{-6})(\pi)(0.03)}{(0.106 \times 10^{-3})(0.01)} = 0.00711\,\Omega$$

$$\text{Power } P_w = I_c^2 R = (500)^2(0.00711) = 1.78 \text{ kW}$$

Comparison with the exponential distributions of current, field strength and power, which result from the idealised, uniform, lossless situation:

1. Resistivity increases with temperature. Current is reduced in the hotter, outer region and penetrates further into the inner, cooler region. Power density is correspondingly modified.

2. Below Curie temperature permeability effectively falls with increasing field strength due to saturation. It is therefore lowest at the surface and increases with depth. The reduced value implies greater skin depth and a redistribution of current and power density, from outer to inner region, as above.

3. Permeability falls to unity when Curie temperature is reached. This occurs initially in the outer layer. Consequently, power density falls there and increases in the layer below. In this way, heating is concentrated in a zone which transfers progressively deeper into the material.

4. The surface temperature is reduced by heat loss, so that the highest temperature occurs a little below the surface.

IH3

An expression for the current density J at depth y in a semi-infinite conductor is:

$$J(y) = \hat{J}_0 e^{-ay}.\cos(\omega t - ay)$$

What are the practical implications of this relationship?

Prove or justify the expression for loss density or power dissipation of the form

$$\text{Loss density} = \frac{\rho.H_m^{\,2}}{2\delta}$$

Define the symbols and units.

Calculate the loss density of low carbon steel from the following data:

$$\text{Resistivity} = 20 \times 10^{-8} \text{ ohm metres at } 20\,^{\circ}\text{C}$$

$$\mu_r = 500$$

$$\text{Field} = 100{,}000 \text{ Am}^{-1} \text{ (peak)}$$

$$\text{Frequency} = 50 \text{ Hz}$$

(Electroheat Tutorials)

Solution

At the surface J is a maximum and in phase with the field. At any other depth J falls off exponentially and at a phase angle to the surface field. When $y = \dfrac{1}{a}$ J is e^{-1} times its surface value and this depth is called the 'depth of penetration' δ. Most of the power is absorbed in one skin depth (86%).

$$\delta = \sqrt{\frac{2\rho}{\mu\omega}} = \sqrt{\left(\frac{2 \times 20 \times 10^{-8}}{500 \times 4\pi \times 10^{-7} \times 2\pi \times 50}\right)}$$

$$= 1.42 \text{ mm}$$

$$\text{Loss density} = \frac{\rho \hat{H}^2}{2\delta}$$

$$= \frac{20 \times 10^{-8} \times 10^{10}}{2 \times 1.42 \times 10^{-3}}$$

$$= 0.7 \text{ MW m}^{-2}$$

IH4

A steel slab 25 mm thick is heated on both sides at a power density of 1 MW/m². Estimate the time taken to raise the mean temperature from 20 to 1000 °C given $(c\gamma) \doteqdot 5 \times 10^6 \dfrac{J}{m^3 K}$.

Given thermal conductivity of $k = 30 \text{ Wm}^{-1}\text{ K}^{-1}$ find the centre to surface temperature difference.

What would happen for a steel slab 100 mm thick?

(Reference 44)

Solution

For the 25 mm slab

$$t = \frac{\theta_m . b . (c\gamma)}{2P} = \frac{(1000 - 20).(0.025).5 \times 10^6}{2 \times 1.0 \times 10^6}$$

$$= 60 \text{ sec.} \quad [1 \text{ MW/m}^2 \text{ into '1 inch' takes 1 minute}]$$

$$(\theta_s - \theta_c) = \frac{P.b}{4k} = \frac{1 \times 10^6 \times 0.025}{4 \times 30}$$

$$= 208°C \quad \left[\theta_s = \theta_m + \frac{P.b}{k.6} = 980 + 139 = 1119 °C \right]$$

$$\text{also } \tau = \frac{k.t}{(c\gamma)b^2} = \frac{30 \times 60}{5 \times 10^6 \times 0.025^2} = 0.6$$

ie $\tau > 0.25$. $\therefore$ *steady distribution reached.*

For the 100 mm slab

$$t = \frac{980.(0.1).5 \times 10^6}{2 \times 1.0 \times 10^6} = 246 \text{ seconds to reach } 980 °C$$

$$\theta_s - \theta_c = 832°C$$

$$\text{and } \theta_s = 980 + 556 = 1556 °C \quad \text{SLAB MELTS}$$

$$\text{also } \tau = \frac{kt}{(c\gamma).b^2} = \frac{30 \times 246}{5 \times 10^6 \times (0.1)^2} = 0.15$$

and 'steady state' has still to be reached.

IH5

The expression for power absorbed in a cylindrical workpiece heated by induction is given by the expression

$$P = \mu.\pi.f.H^2. \times \text{workpiece volume} \times p$$

μ is permeability, H is surface (coil) field strength A/m, f is applied frequency Hz and $p = \dfrac{2}{\left[1.23 + \dfrac{d}{\delta} \right]}$ d is workpiece diameter (m), δ is depth of penetration (m).

Assuming $\dfrac{d}{\delta} \gg 8$ show that the power density P' is given by:

$$P' = \frac{\rho.H^2}{2\delta}$$

(Electroheat Tutorials — the author)

Solution

$$P' = \frac{P}{\pi.d.h}. \quad \text{Cylinder diameter } d, \text{ height } h.$$

$$P = \mu.\pi.f.H^2.\left(\frac{h.\pi.d^2}{4} \right).\frac{2\delta}{d}$$

68

$$\therefore \quad P' = (\mu \pi f).H^2.\frac{d}{4}.2\frac{\delta}{d} \quad \text{and} \quad \delta^2 = \frac{2\rho}{\mu\omega}$$

$$= \frac{\rho}{\delta^2}.H^2.\frac{\delta}{2}$$

$$= \frac{\rho H^2}{2\delta}$$

IH6

Discuss the striation phenomenon.

To avoid striation when heating a workpiece width greater than ten times the skin depth a frequency f must be used so that

$$f \geqslant \frac{10^5}{d^2} \text{ Hz where } d \text{ is heated thickness in mm.}$$

A flat single turn coil fed at 500 k Hz surrounds a mild steel cylindrical workpiece. The diameter of the workpiece is 1 cm and its length 5 cm. (The applied power* can rise to 20 kW.)

Find the depth of penetration at 20 °C and 1000 °C. Determine if striation occurs and its nodal distance below 500 °C if the cylinder is to be case-hardened to about 1 mm.

$$[\mu_r = 500; \ \mu = 4\pi \times 10^{-7}; \ C_{steel} = 5 \times 10^3 \text{ m/sec}]$$

$$\rho_{20} = 0.16 \times 10^{-6} \, \Omega\text{m}; \ \rho_{1000} = 1.2 \times 10^{-6} \, \Omega\text{m}$$

(The author)

Solution

First part summarised in Industrial Applications of Induction Heating by Lozinskii, Pergamon Press, 1969 pp. 38-42.[41]

The workpiece length is greater than ten times the heated depth.

$$\delta_{20\,°C} = \sqrt{\frac{\rho}{\mu.\pi.f}} = \sqrt{\frac{0.16 \times 10^{-6}}{500 \times 4\pi \times 10^{-7} \times \pi \times 5.0 \times 10^5}}$$

$$= 0.0127 \text{ mm}$$

$$\delta_{1000\,°C} = \sqrt{\frac{1.2 \times 10^{-6}}{4\pi 10^{-7} \times \pi \times 5.0 \times 10^5}}$$

$$= 0.769 \text{ mm.}$$

For case-hardening

$$f \geqslant \frac{10^5}{d^2} = \frac{10^5}{1} \text{ or } 100 \text{ k Hz for the particular case}$$

---

*Applied power given to prove: $\Delta\rho > \dfrac{1000 \text{ W}}{5 \times 0.769} (= 260 \text{ W}).$

but at 20 °C heated thickness is 0.0127 initially and

$$f \geqslant \frac{10^5}{(0.012)^2} = 694 \, \text{MHz}$$

so striation will be expected initially.

The initial nodal distance will be

$$x = \frac{\lambda}{2} = \frac{c}{2f} = \frac{5 \times 10^5}{2 \times 5 \times 10^5} = 0.5 \, \text{cm}$$

IH7

Explain what is meant by 'resonance' in electric circuits and show how power factor correction is closely associated with it.

A medium frequency single phase inductor alternator for an induction heating application is rated at 400 volts, 200 amperes, 5000 Hertz. Its internal impedance consists of 5 Ω inductive reactance and negligible resistance. Show how the effective reactance of the alternator can be reduced to zero by adding an appropriate series capacitor connected permanently between alternator and load. Find the voltage at the alternator terminals when it is supplying a 2-ohm unity power factor load at 200 amperes.

(Courtesy of the University of Newcastle upon Tyne)

Solution

The first part of the question is a standard request for knowledge of R, L, C circuits. However a good student noting the second part of the question might wish to observe that many industrial circuits have leading or lagging power factors and that induction heating is a good example of a circuit with a low (lagging) power factor which will need correction to fully use the power rating of the source supply.

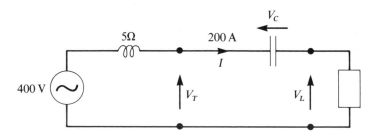

If the terminals of the machine were short-circuited, the alternator would supply a current of 400/5, i.e. 80 A — far short of its rating.

In order to reduce or eliminate the effect of the internal reactance a series capacitor can be added.

For $X_C = 5\,\Omega$, $\dfrac{1}{2\pi f C} = 5$, i.e. $C = \dfrac{1}{2\pi \times 5000 \times 5} = 6.366\,\mu F$.

Now when the load is a $2\,\Omega$ unity power factor load of 200 A, the phasor diagram is as follows

$$\bar{V}_T = \bar{V}_L + \bar{V}_C \quad \text{(sum of phasors)}$$

$$= 400\ \angle 0^\circ + 1000\ \angle -90^\circ$$

$$= 1077\ \angle -68.2^\circ\ \text{V}$$

i.e. terminal voltage $= 1077$ V, lagging I by 68.2°.

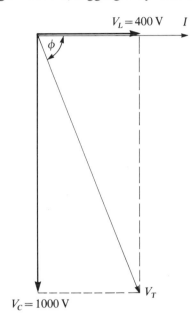

IH8

Discuss the significance of the Curie temperature in inductively heating mild steel slabs. State an expression for the skin depth δ and define each term. Describe the concept of integrated resistivity in heating slabs at wide temperature variations.

Assuming a linear variation of the resistivity, ρ, with temperature T, prove that the integrated resistivity δ_{in} can be expressed as:

$$\rho_{in} = \left[\frac{\sqrt{\rho_1} + \sqrt{\rho_2}}{4} \right]^2$$

where ρ_1 and ρ_2 are the resistivities at temperatures T_1 and T_2 respectively. Semi-infinite slab theory may be assumed where the power dissipated per square metre of surface P is given by $H_0^2 \rho / 2\delta$ where H_0 is the peak magnetising field.

A mild steel slab of 40 mm in depth is to be heated from $20\,^\circ$C to a temperature of $1250\,^\circ$C. If the frequency of operation up to the

Curie temperature (760°) is 50 Hz, determine the minimum frequency needed above the Curie point if the power density there does not drop below 50% of that below the Curie point.

Assume the magnetising field H_0 to be the same throughout the heating temperature range.

The effective permeability of steel between ambient and Curie temperatures may be assumed constant and equal to 400. Linear relationships between resistivity and temperature in the regions 20 °C to 760 °C and 760 °C to 1250 °C may also be assumed.

Data: The resistivities at 20 °C, 760 °C and 1250 °C are $16 \times 10^{-7}\,\Omega\text{m}$, $102 \times 10^{-6}\,\Omega\text{m}$ and $1.23 \times 10^{-6}\,\Omega\text{m}$ respectively.

(*Electroheat Tutorials — Cambridge University*)

Solution

(i) *Theoretical part*

The skin depth or field penetration depth relates to the reduction of the fields (electric or magnetic) within the material, i.e. if $\hat{H} = \hat{H}_0 e^{j\omega t}$ is the applied field, the field developed in the metal is given by

$$H = H_0 e^{-Y/\delta} \cos(\omega t - Y/\delta)$$

The skin depth is δ and is given by

$$\delta = \frac{2\rho}{\mu_o \mu_r \delta \omega}$$

where ρ is the resistivity, μ_r is the relative permeability and $\omega = 2\pi f$ is the angular frequency.

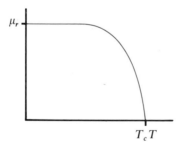

As the Curie temperature is approached steel becomes non-magnetic and $\mu_r \to 1$. The physical mechanisms and the effect on the magnetic field and current density and power density, P, is very complex. Basically as the temperature of the surface reaches the Curie temperature, P reduces but inside where the steel is still magnetic P is still high. The resistivity varies which also changes the power density at every depth. The billet becomes non-magnetic as each layer reaches T_c. To account for the drop of P after the Curie point is reached it is usual practice (assuming economic factors are favourable) to change to a higher frequency.

The resistivity rises with temperature. In calculations involving a wide temperature range the resistivity can be assumed linear within given ranges. If that is so a new value of the resistivity can be assumed which relates to the two spot resistivities defining the linear range. The new value is called integrated resistivity and is assumed constant within the said range.

We assume that

$$\frac{dT}{dt} = A.\sqrt{\rho} \quad \text{since} \quad P = H_o{}^2 \cdot \frac{\rho}{\delta} = A_o\sqrt{\rho}.$$

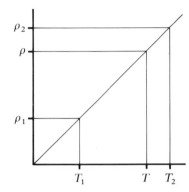

where A and A_o are constants.

$$\frac{\rho - \rho_1}{\rho_2 - \rho_1} = \frac{T - T_1}{T_2 - T_1} \quad \text{and} \quad \rho = \rho_1 + \left[\frac{\rho_2 - \rho_1}{T_2 - T_1}\right] \cdot (T - T_1).$$

Therefore

$$\int_{T_1}^{T_2} \frac{dT}{A\sqrt{\rho}} = \int_0^t dt = \int_{T_1}^{T_2} \frac{dT}{A\sqrt{\rho_{in}}}$$

Consider the first integral

$$\frac{1}{A} \int_{T_1}^{T_2} \frac{dT}{\left(\rho_1 \times \left(\frac{\rho_2 - \rho_1}{T_2 - T_1}\right).(T - T_1)\right)^{1/2}} = \frac{1}{A} \int_{T_1}^{T_2} \frac{dT}{\sqrt{B.T + C}}$$

$$= \frac{2}{AB} \cdot \left[\sqrt{BT + C}\right]_{T_1}^{T_2} = \frac{2}{AB} \cdot \left[\sqrt{\rho_1 + \left[\frac{\rho_2 - \rho_1}{T_2 - T_1}\right](T - T_1)}\right]_{T_1}^{T_2}$$

$$\text{where} \quad B = \frac{\rho_2 - \rho_1}{T_2 - T_1} \quad \text{and} \quad C = -\left[\frac{\rho_2 - \rho_1}{T_2 - T_1}\right] \cdot T_1 + \rho_1$$

$$= \frac{2}{AB} \cdot [\sqrt{\rho_2} - \sqrt{\rho_1}]$$

$$= \frac{2}{A}\left[\frac{(T_2 - T_1)}{(\rho_2 - \rho_1)} \cdot [\sqrt{\rho_2} - \sqrt{\rho_1}]\right].$$

But

$$\int_{T_1}^{T_2} \frac{dT}{A\sqrt{\rho_{in}}} = \frac{(T_2 - T_1)}{A\sqrt{\rho_{in}}} = \frac{2}{A}\left[\frac{(T_2 - T_1)}{(\rho_2 - \rho_1)}\right] \cdot [\sqrt{\rho_2} - \sqrt{\rho_1}].$$

$$\therefore \quad \sqrt{\rho_{in}} = \frac{1}{2}\left[\frac{\rho_2 - \rho_1}{\sqrt{\rho_2} - \sqrt{\rho_1}}\right] = \frac{1}{2}\left[\frac{(\sqrt{\rho_2} - \sqrt{\rho_1})(\sqrt{\rho_1} + \sqrt{\rho_2})}{\sqrt{\rho_2} - \sqrt{\rho_1}}\right]$$

and $\quad \sqrt{\rho_{in}} = \frac{1}{2}[\sqrt{\rho_2} + \sqrt{\rho_1}] \quad$ or $\quad \rho_{in} = \frac{[\sqrt{\rho_2} + \sqrt{\rho_1}]^2}{4} \quad$ QED

(ii) *Numerical part*

The integrated resistivities: in $20°$ to $760°C$ range REGION (1)

$$\rho_{in_1} = \frac{10^{-8}}{4}(\sqrt{16} + \sqrt{102})^2 = 4.97 \times 10^{-7} \, \Omega m$$

and within 760 to $1250°C$ REGION (2)

$$\rho_{in_2} = \frac{10^{-8}}{4} \cdot (\sqrt{102} + \sqrt{123})^2 = 1.12 \times 10^{-6} \, \Omega m$$

But

$$P = \frac{H_0}{2} \cdot \frac{\rho}{\delta} = \text{Constant} \sqrt{\frac{\mu}{r} \times f \times \rho_{in}}$$

If in region 2

$$P_2 \geqslant \frac{P_1}{2}$$

then

$$\sqrt{\frac{\mu}{r_1} \times f_1 \times \rho_{in_1}} \leqslant \sqrt{\frac{\mu}{r_2} \times f_2 \times \rho_{in_2}} \times 2$$

Giving

$$f_2 \geqslant \frac{f_1}{4} \cdot \frac{\rho_{in_1}}{\rho_{in_2}} \cdot \frac{\mu_1}{\mu_2} = \frac{50}{4} \times 400 \times \frac{4.97}{11.2}$$

If $f_1 = 50 \, Hz$ then $f_2 \geqslant 2.2 \, kHz$.

IH9

A cylindrical steel billet is 60 mm long and 30 mm in diameter. At $20°C$ it has the following parameter values: a relative permeability of 200, a resistivity of $0.4 \, \mu\Omega m$ and a temperature coefficient of resistance of 0.0057 per $°C$. It is heated by an induction coil having 6 turns, and supplied with current at 150 Hz. Determine the current required in the coil for a billet temperature of $450°C$, to produce the same rate of heat generation in the billet as a coil current of 1.5 kA at a billet temperature of $20°C$. State any necessary assumptions.

$$\text{Skin depth } \delta = \sqrt{\frac{2\rho}{\mu\omega}}$$

where ρ is resistivity, μ is permeability and ω is angular frequency.

Describe how an almost uniform temperature is achieved during the heating of a steel billet by induction heating. Explain also how this is prevented for a surface-heating application.

(Courtesy of Huddersfield Polytechnic)

Solution

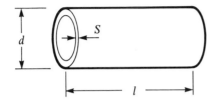

Heat rate generation is $P = I_s^2 R$ where steel current $I_s = 6I_p$ and $R = \dfrac{\rho l}{A}$ of annulus around circumference. For equal rate of heat generation for the two cases:

$$P_1 = P_2 \quad \therefore \quad I_{s1}^2 R_1 = I_{s2}^2 R_2$$

$$\therefore \quad I_{p_1}^2 R_1 = I_{p_2}^2 R_2$$

but

$$R = \frac{\rho \pi d}{\delta l}; \quad I_{p_1}^2 \cdot \frac{\rho_1 \pi d}{\delta_1 l} = \frac{I_{p_2}^2 \cdot \rho_2 \pi d}{\delta_2 l}$$

Assume all I flows in one skin depth

$$I_{p_2}^2 = I_{p_1}^2 \frac{\rho_1}{\rho_2} \cdot \frac{\delta_2}{\delta_1}$$

But

$$\rho_2 = \rho_1(1 + \alpha t)$$

and

$$\delta = \sqrt{\frac{2\rho}{\mu\omega}}$$

$$I_{p_2}^2 = I_{p_1}^2 \frac{\rho_1}{\rho_2} \left[\frac{\rho_2}{\rho_1} \right]^{1/2}$$

$$= I_{p_1}^2 \frac{\sqrt{1 + \alpha t}}{(1 + \alpha t)}$$

$$I_{p_2}^2 = I_{p_1}^2 / \sqrt{1 + \alpha t}$$

Assume that α and μ_r are constant

$$1 + \alpha t = 1 + 0.0057.430 = 1 + 2.45 = 3.45$$

$$I_{p_2}^2 = 1500^2 / \sqrt{3.45} = 1.21.10^6$$

$$\therefore \quad I_{p_2} = 1100 \text{ A}$$

75

Note: a solution can also be attempted by the following route.

For transformer with a single-turn secondary

$$I_{s1} = 1500 \cdot \tfrac{6}{1} = 9 \, \text{kA}$$

Heat generation rate

$$P_1 = I_{s1}{}^2 R_1$$

$$R_1 = \frac{\rho_1 l}{A} = \frac{0.4.10^{-6}\pi.30.10^{-3}}{60.10^{-3}.\delta_1} = \frac{0.628.10^{-6}}{\delta_1}$$

$$\delta_1 = \sqrt{\frac{2\rho_1}{\mu\omega}} = \sqrt{\frac{2 \times 0.4 \times 10^{-6}}{200 \times 4\pi 10^{-7} \times 2\pi 150}} = \sqrt{3.38.10^{-6}}$$

$$\delta_1 = 1.84 \, \text{mm}$$

$$R_1 = \frac{0.628.10^{-6}}{1.84.10^{-3}} = 0.341 \, \text{m}\Omega$$

$$P_1 = 9^2.10^6 \times 0.341 \times 10^{-3} = 27.6 \, \text{kW}$$

For the same rate of heat generation $P_2 = 27.6 \, \text{kW}$. Also

$$\rho_2 = \rho_1(1 + \alpha t)$$
$$= 0.4(1 + 0.0057.430) = 0.4(1 + 2.45)$$
$$= 0.4 \times 3.45$$
$$= 1.38 \, \mu\Omega\text{m}$$

$$\delta_2 = \sqrt{\frac{2 \times 1.38 \times 10^{-6}}{200 \times 4\pi 10^{-7} \times 2\pi 150}} = \sqrt{11.65 \times 10^{-6}}$$

$$\delta_2 = 3.41 \, \text{mm}$$

$$R_2 = \frac{1.38 \times 10^{-6}.\pi.30 \times 10^{-3}}{60.10^{-3} \times 3.41.10^{-3}} = 0.64 \, \text{m}\Omega$$

$$I_{s2}^2 = P_2/R_2 = \frac{27.6 \times 10^3}{0.64 \times 10^{-3}} = 43.13 \times 10^6$$

$$\therefore \quad I_{s2} = 6.57 \, \text{kA}$$

$$I_{p2} = \frac{6.32}{6} = 1094 \, \text{A}$$

Assumed α and μ_r are constant and all I_s flows in one skin depth δ.

The second part follows from the earlier calculations. Initially, most of heat generated in one skin depth. As steel heats up (in δ),

76

resistivity (ρ) increases which forces current deeper. This results in radial variation in ρ and more even radial heating. μ_r also decreases as temperature increases, thus increasing the skin depth δ or helping to push current deeper.

At the Curie point ($\doteqdot 600\,°\mathrm{C}$ steel) μ_r becomes unity producing a much larger depth of penetration. Heat is lost to the surroundings from the outer surface and heat is conducted internally towards centre of the workpiece both of which create a more even radial temperature profile.

Surface treatment
Uniform radial temperature is prevented by:

i) high frequency which keeps the skin depth small, concentrating the heat generation into the surface layer.

ii) applying for a short time, this prevents conduction of heat to centre (and to the outside),

iii) a high current or power density may be used to concentrate heat into the surface layer.

IH10

i In the context of induction heating, describe the STRIATION phenomenon. Why does it occur?

ii An induction heater has a coil of 15 turns operating at 60 kHz and 80 A. It is used to case harden a cylindrical steel workpiece of length 25 cm. Given that the steel's relative permeability is 120, and resistivity is $5 \times 10^{-6}\,\Omega\mathrm{m}$, calculate the diameter of the workpiece if the power input is 0.14 MW. Assume no transformer losses, that there are no heat losses from the workpiece and that all the workpiece current is confined within the depth of penetration (δ).

iii A cylindrical steel workpiece is heated at a constant rate of 75 kW/m² for 120 seconds. The characteristics of the steel cylinder are:

Length	30 cm
Diameter	12 cm
μ_r (relative permeability)	150
ρ_r (resistivity)	$5 \times 10^{-6} \times \Omega\mathrm{m}$
ρ_D (density)	$7.8 \times 10^3\ \mathrm{kg/m^3}$
C_p (specific heat capacity)	$0.5\dfrac{\mathrm{kJ}}{\mathrm{kg\,K}}$

After 120 seconds the power is disconnected and the cylinder allowed to 'SOAK', i.e. its temperature distribution is allowed to settle. If there are NO heat losses from the cylinder, calculate its new steady-state temperature. (Its starting temperature is taken as 12 °C.)

$$\mu_o = 4\pi \times 10^{-7} \text{ Henry/metre}$$

(*Courtesy of the University of Aston*)

Solution

i)   The striation phenomenon exhibits itself as uneven heating particularly of heated metallic surfaces facing excited heating coils. The phenomenon acts as a limiting effect in heating processes where there is no time for temperature equalisation (soaking) between the heating and working. Striation is a function of applied frequency and workpiece dimensions (thickness) leading inferentially from power density.

There are empirical limits and by way of example, for most metallic cylinders the effect of striation will not occur if

$$f \geqslant \frac{10^5}{d^2} \text{ Hz where } d \text{ is the diameter}$$

The literature has not explored the theoretical limitations of most geometries in a satisfactory manner.

The phenomenon is due to the presence of standing waves usually with steel placed in an alternating electromagnetic field. This field will cause a sympathetic vibration between nodes dictated by applied frequency, the steel dimensions and its physical and magnetic properties. These properties will vary between the nodes thus enhancing heating non-uniformity.

ii)   The resistance of the workpiece is given by

$$R_w = \frac{0.14 \times 10^6}{(80 \times 15)^2}$$

$$= 9.72 \times 10^{-2} \text{ ohms.}$$

This resistance occurs over an active volume of a length given by the cylinder's circumference and the area by the product of the cylinder's length and the active depth of penetration δ.

Generally

$$\delta = \sqrt{\frac{2.\rho}{\mu_0 . \mu_r . \omega}}$$

now

$$\omega = 2.\pi.60.10^3$$

$$\therefore \quad \delta = \sqrt{\frac{2 \times 5 \times 10^{-6}}{4\pi \times 10^{-7} \times 120 \times 2\pi \times 60 \times 10^3}}$$

$$= 4.19 \times 10^{-4}\,\text{m}$$

Thus

$$R_w = \frac{\rho \times \pi \times D}{\delta \times l}$$

from which

$$D = \frac{R.\delta.l}{\rho.\pi}$$

$$= \frac{9.72 \times 10^{-2} \times 4.19 \times 10^{-4} \times 0.25}{5 \times 10^{-6} \times \pi}$$

$$= 0.65\,\text{m}$$

iii)   The heat content of the workpiece is given by the expression

$$Q = P \times \text{surface area} \times t = m \times C_p \times \delta T$$

$$P = \text{surface power density}$$

$$t = \text{time}$$

$$m = \text{workpiece mass}$$

$$C_p = \text{specific heat}$$

$$\delta T = \text{temperature rise}$$

$$\theta_m = \text{workpiece temperature}$$

This ignores thermal losses

$$\delta T = (\theta_m - 12)$$

$$\theta_m = \frac{P \times \pi \times D \times L \times t}{\dfrac{\pi.D^2}{4} \times L \times \rho_D \times C_p} + 12$$

$$= \frac{4 \times 75 \times 10^3 \times 120}{0.113 \times 7.8 \times 10^3 \times 0.5 \times 10^3} + 12$$

$$= 93.7^\circ\text{C}$$

IH11

List the factors which influence the power input to an inductively heated load.

Some preliminary tests were carried out before finalising an arrangement for annealing brass cartridge cups. The surface temperature of a cup was measured during the heating time for two different operator output levels (A and B), each sufficient to ensure that the cup reached the annealing temperature of 700 °C. The temperature-time relationships are shown in Fig. IH11 with the final temperatures achieved.

The power input to the generator was also measured in each case and was found to be 1.05 kW and 1.90 kW respectively. The work coil was then disconnected from the generator and its resistance and inductance were measured at the nominal operating frequency of the generator of 1 MHz first without the cup and then with the cup inside the work coil. The measured values were 0.15 Ω and 0.9 μH without the cup and whilst no appreciable change in inductance was observed the resistance with the cup was 0.35 Ω. For a cup surface area of $69 \times 10^{-4} \, \text{m}^2$, radiation constant of $5.73 \times 10^{-8} \, \text{W} \, \text{m}^{-2} \, \text{K}^{-4}$ and ambient temperature of 20 °C, select the most suitable heating rates, A or B of Fig. IH11, justifying your choice.

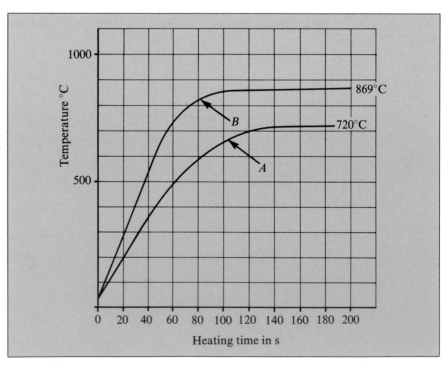

Figure IH11

Calculate also:

a) the overall efficiency of the installation

b) the transfer efficiency of the work coil and estimate an upper limit

c) the power factor of the load presented to the generator terminals.

If the tank coil inductance and resistance, excluding the work coil, are $9\,\mu H$ and $0.1\,\Omega$ and the oscillator has been designed for an optimum loaded Q value of 25, show that the induction generator is not adequately loaded and suggest a way of overcoming this.

You may asume that the average conductivity for copper is five times that for brass.

(*Courtesy of NELP. (B.Sc. Finals, 1977*))

Solution

Factors which should be mentioned include the work coil ampere turns, the permeability and resistivity of the material being heated, the operating frequency of the generator, the degree of coupling between the work and coil and the radius and length of the work (or workpiece volume).

If P_A and P_B are the power inputs to the work for heating rate A and heating rate B respectively the energy inputs required to reach $700\,°C$ are

$$P_A \times 58\ \text{W.s} \quad \text{and} \quad P_B \times 132\ \text{W.s.}$$

Now

$$P_B = 5.73 \times 10^{-8} \times 69 \times 10^{-4}(1142^4 - 293^4) = 670\ \text{W}$$

$$P_A = 5.73 \times 10^{-8} \times 69 \times 10^{-4}(993^4 - 293^4) = 381\ \text{W}$$

hence

$$P_B \times 58 = 670 \times 58 = 39\ \text{kW seconds}$$

$$P_A \times 132 = 381 \times 132 = 50\ \text{kW seconds}$$

Hence heating rate B is best because the energy input is less and in addition production rate will be increased.

$$\text{The overall efficiency} = \frac{670}{1900} = 35\%$$

$$\text{The transfer efficiency of the coil} = \frac{\Delta R_1}{R + \Delta R_1} = \frac{0.35 - 0.15}{0.35} = 57\%.$$

Since conductivity for copper is 5 times that of brass the maximum possible efficiency is

$$\frac{1}{1+\sqrt{\frac{1}{5}}}=69\%$$

Input to work coil + brass cup $= \dfrac{670}{0.59} = 1136$ W.

The coil current $I = \sqrt{\dfrac{1136}{0.35}} = 57$ A.

If V is the voltage across the coil terminals and the resistance of the coil is neglected

$$VI = \omega(L-\Delta L)I^2 = 2\pi \times 10^6 \times 0.9 \times 10^{-6} \times 57^2 = 18.4 \text{ k.V.I.}$$

Capacitance in picafarad $= \dfrac{1136}{18,400} = 0.062.$

The loaded Q of the tank circuit is $\dfrac{2\pi \times 10^6 \times 9.9 \times 10^{-6}}{0.35+0.1} = 138.$

This is in excess of the design value and therefore the generator is not adequately loaded. If the work is coupled to the generator through a transformer, the load presented to this generator is increased.

Dielectric heating

CHAPTER 5

5.1. Background to the teaching

In this group the topics of radio frequency and micro-wave heating
are considered. The frequencies employed are specified by
regulation and in the UK centre on 13.56 MHz and 27.12 MHz (rf)
and 896 MHz and 2450 MHz (microwave).

In its simplest form dielectric heating may be represented as the
exploitation of the loss mechanism in a capacitive circuit. Thus the
subject can be approached by two distinct methods using circuit
analysis and wave propagation and transmission. The latter
approach tends to be mathematical and for the generic cases is to
be preferred. The former approach becomes rapidly empirical and
tends to be employed in specific situations when practical
considerations are well understood. A convenient summary of
volumetric heating is given in reference 2. A helpful summary
review of the fundamentals occurs in reference 45.

Reference 2 also provides a most convenient list of references but
perhaps the fundamental reference is still that due to Von Hippel[46].
Lesson 4 of reference 6 provides an interesting background.

The subject may be taught by examining polarisation and
conductivity effects leading to the determination of power
dissipation in poor conductors arranged in capacitor form. A
review of the dielectric properties of materials and elementary
components of rf and microwave circuits gives a helpful
background to common applications in the fields of moisture
levelling (the drying and reduction of moisture fluctuations) in
textiles and plastics welding. A separate review of power supplies
for both rf and microwave supplies is recommended.

It has been found helpful to consider the subject after treating
conductive heating and can be a convenient exploitation of the
unified approach[21] emphasising the higher frequencies. To those
wishing, however, to restrict their consideration to the higher
frequencies there are many good textbooks. Perhaps because of its
identity with reference 14 the textbook by Baden-Fuller[47] will be
found useful.

5.2. The worked examples

DH1

Assuming that the electric field, in one dimension of a plane wave propagating through a medium with a propagation constant γ is given by

$$E(y, t) = E_0 e^{j\omega t} e^{-\gamma \cdot y}$$

prove that this satisfies the wave equation in one dimension

$$\frac{\partial^2 E}{\partial y^2} = \varepsilon_0 K \mu \frac{\partial^2 E}{\partial t^2}$$

and find an expression for γ. ε_0 is the permittivity of free space, μ is the medium permeability (assumed real) and the parameter K is given by

$$K = \varepsilon' - j\left(\varepsilon'' + \frac{\sigma}{\omega \varepsilon_0}\right)$$

where ε' is the dielectric constant, ε'' is the loss factor, σ is the conductivity of the medium and μ is the angular frequency.

Show that for a metallic material $\gamma = (1 + j)/\delta$ and find an expression for δ in terms of ω, μ and σ. Calculate δ for low carbon mild steel at 50 Hz and 500 Hz taking $\sigma = 10^8/20$ mho/m, $\mu = \mu_0 \mu_r$, where $\mu_0 = 4\pi \times 10^{-7}$ Hm^{-1} and $\mu_r = 500$.

(Electroheat Tutorial — Cambridge University)

Solution

Strictly speaking the example relates to conductive heating but it is included as a good example of the unified approach[21], the theoretical part and the upper frequency used being the applicable components to this topic grouping.

$$\frac{\partial E}{\partial y} = -\gamma . E(y, t); \qquad \frac{\partial E}{\partial t} = j.\omega E(y, t)$$

$$\frac{\partial^2 E}{\partial y^2} = \gamma^2 . E(y, t); \qquad \frac{\partial^2 E}{\partial t^2} = -\omega^2 E(y, t)$$

The left hand side of the wave equation becomes:

$$\frac{\partial^2 E}{\partial y^2} = \gamma^2 . E.(y, t)$$

The right hand side of the wave equation becomes:

$$\varepsilon_0 . K . \mu . \frac{\partial^2 E}{\partial t^2} = \varepsilon_0 . K . \mu . [-\omega^2 . E(y, t)]$$

For the wave equation to be satisfied by $E(y, t) = E_0 . e^{j\omega t} . e^{-\gamma \cdot y}$, then

$$\gamma^2 = -\omega^2 . \mu . \varepsilon_0 . K$$

and

$$\gamma = j.\omega.[\mu.\varepsilon_0.K]^{1/2}$$

Noting

$$K = \varepsilon' - j.\left[\varepsilon'' + \frac{\sigma}{\omega.\varepsilon_0}\right]$$

then for a metal (a good conductor) $\varepsilon' = 0$ and $\varepsilon'' = 0$

$$\therefore \quad K = \left[\frac{-j.\sigma}{\omega.\varepsilon_0}\right]$$

so that

$$\gamma^2 = -\omega^2.\mu.\varepsilon_0.\left[\frac{-j.\sigma}{\omega.\varepsilon_0}\right]$$

$$= j.\sigma.\omega.\mu$$

Now

$$\sqrt{2.j} = (1+j)$$

so that

$$\gamma = \left[\frac{\sigma.\omega.\mu}{2}\right]^{1/2}.\sqrt{2j}$$

Putting

$$\delta = \sqrt{\frac{2}{\sigma.\omega\mu}}$$

Then

$$\gamma = (1+j)/\delta \qquad\qquad \text{QED}$$

At 50 Hz

$$\delta = \sqrt{\frac{2}{(10^8/20) \times 2.\pi.50 \times 500 \times 4 \times \pi \times 10^{-7}}}$$

$$= 1.42 \times 10^{-3} \text{ metres } (1.42 \text{ mm})$$

At 500 Hz

$$\delta = \sqrt{\frac{2}{(10^8/20) \times 2.\pi.500.1000 \times 500 \times 4 \times \pi \times 10^7}}$$

$$= 1.42 \times 10^{-5} \text{ metres } (0.0142 \text{ mm})$$

DH2

Starting from the average power developed in a dielectric medium

$$P_{av} = \tfrac{1}{2}\omega\varepsilon_0\varepsilon_{eff}{}'' \int_V \hat{E}.\hat{E}^* dV$$

develop an expression for the average power in a water cylindrical dielectric of height h and radius R placed axially in a cylindrical microwave cavity operating at 900 MHz. Hence deduce an equivalent average field E_{av} established within the dielectric and show that

$$E_{av} = E_m J_0(kR)\left[1 + \frac{J_0'^2(kR)}{J_0{}^2(kR)}\right]^{1/2}$$

where E_m is the RMS value of the field axial variation at $r=0$.

Calculate the ratio E_{av}/E_m for water ($\varepsilon' = 80$) with $R = 3.5$ mm. Assume the field in the cavity varies as $E = E_m J_0(kr)$ where $k = \omega\sqrt{\varepsilon_0\mu_0\varepsilon'}$, and the integral

$$\int_0^R r J_0{}^2[k.r]dr = \left[\frac{r^2}{2}.(J_0{}^2(k.r) + J_0'^2(k.r))\right]_0^R$$

(Electroheat Tutorials — Cambridge University)

Solution

The first part is derived as equation 4.10 in reference 2.

Because $P_{av} = \tfrac{1}{2}.\omega.\varepsilon_0.\varepsilon_{eff}{}''. \int_V \hat{E}.\hat{E}^* dV$ (E in volts/metre).

Then loosely

$$P_{av} = \tfrac{1}{2}.\omega.\varepsilon_0.\varepsilon_{eff}{}''.E_{av}{}^2.(\text{Volume})$$

and in the given case

$$P_{av} = \tfrac{1}{2}.\omega.\varepsilon_0.\varepsilon_{eff}{}''.E_{av}{}^2.\pi.R^2.h$$

But the electric field distribution in the cavity is given as:

$$E = E_m.J_0(k.r)$$

Hence

$$P_{av} = \omega.\varepsilon_0.\varepsilon_{eff}{}''. \int_V E_m{}^2.J_0{}^2(k.r)\,dV$$

$$= \omega.\varepsilon_0.\varepsilon_{eff}{}''.E_m{}^2. \int_0^R J_0{}^2(k.r)\,2\pi r.dr.h$$

(because E_m refers to the $r=0$ axis and $dV = 2\pi r h dr$)

$$P_{av} = \omega.\varepsilon_0.\varepsilon_{eff}''.E_m^2.[2.\pi.h].\int_0^R r.J_0^2(k.r).dr$$

$$= \omega.\varepsilon_0.\varepsilon_{eff}''.E_m^2.[2.\pi.h].\left[\frac{r^2}{2}.(J_0^2(k.r)+J_0'^2(k.r)\right]_0^R$$

$$= \omega.\varepsilon_0.\varepsilon_{eff}''.E_m^2.\pi.h.R^2[J_0^2(k.R)+J_0'^2(k.R)]$$

From which (equating the two separate expressions for P_{av})

$$E_{av} = E_m.J_0(kR).\left[1+\frac{J_0'^2(kR)}{J_0^2(kR)}\right]^{1/2} \qquad \text{QED}$$

Now
$$k = \omega.\sqrt{\varepsilon_0.\mu_0.\varepsilon'}$$

$$= 2.\pi.900.10^6 \times \sqrt{\frac{4.\pi.10^{-7}}{36.\pi.10^9} \times 80}$$

$$= \frac{2\pi 900.10^6}{3 \times 10^8}.\sqrt{80}$$

$$= 168.6$$

and

$$kR = 168.6 \times \frac{3.5}{1000}$$

$$= 0.59$$

From tables

$$J_0(0.59) = 0.91*$$

$$J_0' = (0.59) = 0.28$$

and

$$J_0'(0.59) = \frac{-2 \times 2.249}{9} \cdot (0.59) + \frac{4 \times 1.265}{81} \cdot (0.59)^3$$

$$- \frac{6 \times 0.316}{729} \cdot (0.59)^5 + \dots$$

$$= -0.282$$

$$\frac{E_{av}}{E_m} = 0.91.\left[1+\frac{(-0.28)^2}{(0.91)^2}\right]^{1/2}$$

$$= 0.952$$

---

*Note $J_0(0.59) = 1 - 2.249\left[\frac{0.59}{3}\right]^2 + 1.265\left[\frac{0.59}{3}\right]^4 - 0.316\left[\frac{0.59}{3}\right]^6 + \dots$

$$= 0.911$$

DH3

A lossy load is made up of moist paper sheet 1 mm thick and area 0.01 m² sandwiched between two parallel metallic plates. The complex relative dielectric constant of the paper is given by

$$\varepsilon^* = \varepsilon' - j.\varepsilon'' = 3 - j.0.2$$

Ignoring any conductivity effects, use the expression for the displacement current and show that the lossy load can be represented by a parallel R, C circuit and determine the values of R and C at 27.12 MHz. Derive an expression for the power dissipated per unit volume and calculate the total power in the paper load when an rms field of 1000 kV/m exists across it.
Take $\varepsilon_0 = 8.84 \times 10^{-12}$ F/m.

(*Electroheat Tutorials — Cambridge University*)

Solution
The total current density through the load is (for $E = R_e \hat{E} e^{j\omega t}$, $\hat{E}$ is the peak value of E)

$$J = \sigma E + \varepsilon.\frac{\partial E}{\partial t}$$

Ignoring conductivity term σE then

$$J = \varepsilon_0.\varepsilon^* j.\omega.E = j.\varepsilon_0.\varepsilon'.\omega.\hat{E}.e^{j\omega t} + \omega\varepsilon''.\varepsilon_0.\hat{E}.e^{j\omega t}$$

Using only the real part then

$$J_{\text{actual}} = -\varepsilon_0.\varepsilon'.\omega\hat{E}.\sin\omega t + \omega.\varepsilon_0.\varepsilon''.\hat{E}.\cos\omega t \dots \tag{1}$$

Taking a parallel R/C circuit fed by a periodic voltage $v = R_e \hat{v} e^{j\omega t}$

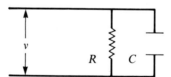

$$J = \frac{v}{R}.\frac{1}{A} + \frac{C}{A}\frac{dv}{dt} = \frac{1}{A}\frac{\hat{v}e^{j\omega t}}{R} + j\frac{C}{A}\omega\hat{v}e^{j\omega t}$$

where A is the plate area and

$$J_{\text{actual}} = \frac{\hat{v}}{R.A}.\cos\omega t - \frac{\omega C}{A}.\hat{v}.\sin\omega t \tag{2}$$

Comparing equations (1) and (2) then:

$$\varepsilon_0.\varepsilon'.\omega.\hat{E} = \omega.C.\hat{v}/A \quad \text{hence} \quad C = \frac{\varepsilon_0.\varepsilon'.A}{d}$$

and

$$\omega.\varepsilon_0.\varepsilon''.E = \frac{\hat{v}}{RA} \quad R = \frac{1}{\omega.\varepsilon''.\varepsilon_0}.\frac{d}{A}$$

where $d\left(=\dfrac{\hat{v}}{E}\right)$ is the separation of the metallic plates.

$$C = \frac{8.84 \times 10^{-12} \times 3 \times 0.01}{10^{-3}} = 265\,\text{pF}$$

$$R = \frac{10^{-3}}{0.01 \times 2 \times \pi \times 27 \times 10^{6} \times 0.2 \times 8.84 \times 10^{-12}} = 333.4\,\Omega$$

Note: $R = \dfrac{\rho.d}{A} = \dfrac{d}{\sigma_{eq}.A}$ and $\sigma_{eq} = \omega\varepsilon_0\varepsilon_r''$ denoting an equivalent conductivity due to the dipolar losses.

Power density is given from Poyntings' theorem.

$$\tfrac{1}{2}R_e[E.J^*] = \tfrac{1}{2}.R_e.(\varepsilon_0(\varepsilon' + j\varepsilon'')).E.(-j).\omega.E$$

$$= \tfrac{1}{2}.\varepsilon_0.\varepsilon''.\omega.\hat{E}^2$$

$$= \varepsilon_0.\varepsilon''.\omega E_{rms}{}^2 = \sigma_{eq}.E_{rms}{}^2$$

Therefore total power into paper

$$= 2 \times \pi \times 27 \times 10^{6} \times 8.84 \times 10^{-12} \times 0.2 \times 0.01$$

$$= 2 \times \pi \times 27 \times 10^{6} \times 8.84 \times 10^{-12} \times 0.2 \times 10^{12} \times 0.01 \times 10^{-3}$$

$$= 3.0\,\text{kW}$$

Note: $\text{Power} = \dfrac{V_{rms}{}^2}{R} = \dfrac{V_{rms}{}^2}{\rho\dfrac{d}{A}} = \sigma_{eq} \times E_{rms}{}^2 \times \text{Volume}$

since $E_{rms} = \dfrac{V_{rms}}{d}$

hence Power/unit volume $= \sigma_{eq}E_{rms}{}^2$

which is the required expression.

DH4

Discuss dielectric heating, stating the essential physical properties of the material to be heated and the relevant design features of such a heater.

A block of plastic 40 cm × 30 cm × 2 cm is heated in a parallel-plate dielectric heater. The plates are in contact with the largest surfaces of the plastic and are supplied at 27.12 MHz at 1.5 kV. The plastic has the following physical properties:

Loss factor: 0.25

Specific heat: 900 J/kg/°C

density: 1200 kg/m³

relative permittivity: 3.0

Calculate

i) the values of the equivalent parallel capacitance and resistance of the load, and

ii) the temperature rise of the plastic after 1.5 minutes.

Describe briefly, with the aid of a block diagram, how the supply for the above heater of plastic is derived.

(Courtesy of University of Aston)

Solution

Dielectrics cannot be heated by the direct resistance or induction mechanisms due to the absence of enough charge carriers, external heating is not possible due to low thermal conductivity (and can burn). Heat produced α f, ε_r, $\tan \delta$, E, f = applied frequency $\varepsilon_r.\tan \delta$ = loss factor, E = applied field.

f must be very high — must keep to international standards
                             — *RF* and microwave

E must be high   — avoid voltage breakdown at sharp edges and in thin materials.

Loss factor $\varepsilon_r.\tan \delta$ varies with frequency and temperature.

If homogeneous and E uniform, then uniform heat generation.

$$C = \varepsilon_0 \varepsilon_r \frac{A}{d} = \frac{8.854 \times 10^{-12} \times 3 \times 0.4 \times 0.3}{0.02} = 159\, pF$$

Loss factor $= \varepsilon_r.\tan \delta$ and $\varepsilon_r = 3$

$$R = \frac{1}{\omega C \tan \delta} = \frac{1}{2\pi \times 27.12 \times 10^6 \times 159 \times 10^{-12} \times 0.25/3} = 443\, \Omega$$

$$E = \frac{1500}{0.02} = 75\, kV/m$$

Heat developed/m^3/s

$$= 2\pi f \varepsilon_0 \varepsilon_r \tan \delta . E^2$$

$$= 2\pi \times 27.12 \times 10^6 \times 8.854 \times 10^{-12} \times 3 \times \frac{0.25}{3} \times 75^2 \times 10^6$$

$$= 2.12\,\mathrm{MW/m^3}$$

Heat developed/m^3 in $1.5\,\mathrm{min} = 2.12 \times 10^6 \times 90 = 191\,\mathrm{MJ/m^3}$

but heat developed $= m \times s \times \Delta T \times \mathrm{Vol}$

$$= \mathrm{density} \times s \times \Delta T$$

$$\therefore \quad \Delta T = \frac{191 \times 10^6}{1200 \times 900} = 177\,^\circ\mathrm{C}$$

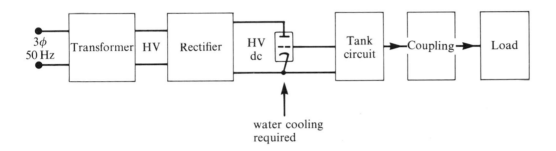

water cooling
required

HV DC obtained by transformation and rectification; thermionic valve supplies oscillatory circuit to produce HF. L and C of tank coupling needs to be included to determine frequency. Automatic tuning needed since load L and C vary during heating.

To transmit maximum power to the load the HF source should always be matched to the load.

DH5

i) Explain what the following terms mean, and their significance:

    a) δ = Depth of penetration in the context of induction heating.

    b) D_p = Penetration depth in the context of microwave heating.

Is there a relationship between them?

ii) The current density of a lossy load within a high frequency electric field is given by:

$$J = j\omega\varepsilon_0 E\varepsilon* \qquad (1)$$

Show how a parallel RC network can be used to represent equation (1). What are the values of R and C in such a network if:

ω = Applied field frequency, $27.12 \times 2\pi$ Mrads/sec

$\hat{E}$ = Applied field strength, 1000 kV/m (peak)

$\varepsilon*$ $= \varepsilon' - j\varepsilon_{eff}''$

$\varepsilon*$ $= 1.1 - j0.05$

ε' = Relative dielectric constant

ε_{eff}'' = Relative loss tangent

ε_0 = Dielectric permeability of free space

    $= 8.85 \times 10^{-12}$ f/m

Area of dielectric load $= 0.01$ m^2

Thickness of dielectric load $= 0.001$ m.

iii) If the expression for power density into the given load is:

$$P_v = \tfrac{1}{2}\mathrm{Re}(J*.E) \qquad (2)$$

calculate the total power into the dielectric.

(NB J and E are vector quantities.)

(*Courtesy of University of Aston 1985*)

Solution

i) *δ — Depth of penetration*
δ is the depth (within the material) at which the current density (J) has dropped to 0.368 of its surface value.

D_p = Penetration depth
D_p is the depth (within the material) at which the field strength or power density reaches 0.368 of its surface value.

$$D_p = \frac{K.\delta}{2}$$

(Related by attenuation factor K for a given material and applied field.)

ii)
$$J = j.\omega.\varepsilon_0.E.\varepsilon*$$

$$= j\omega_0 E(\varepsilon' - j\varepsilon_{eff}'')$$

$$J = \omega.\varepsilon_0.\varepsilon_{eff}''.E + j.\omega.\varepsilon_0.\varepsilon'.E$$

but
$$E = \hat{E}e^{j\omega t}$$

$$J = \omega.\varepsilon_0.\varepsilon_{eff}''.\hat{E}.e^{j\omega t} + j.\omega.\varepsilon_0\varepsilon'.\hat{E}.e^{j\omega t}$$

Taking the Real part (R_e)

$$R_e(J) = \omega.\varepsilon_0.\varepsilon_{eff}''.\hat{E}.\cos \omega t - \omega.\varepsilon_0.\varepsilon'.\hat{E} \sin \omega t \qquad (1)$$

Consider the parallel RC circuit with an input voltage of $\hat{V}e^{j\omega t}$

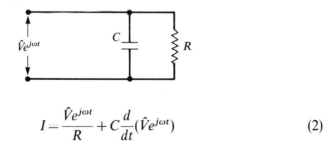

$$I = \frac{\hat{V}e^{j\omega t}}{R} + C\frac{d}{dt}(\hat{V}e^{j\omega t}) \qquad (2)$$

$$J = \frac{I}{A} \quad \text{(where } A = \text{cross sectional area of load (lossy capacitor))}$$

$$J = \frac{\hat{V}}{RA}e^{j\omega t} + J\frac{C}{A}\hat{V}e^{j\omega t}$$

$$R_e(J) = \frac{\hat{V}}{RA}\cos \omega t - \frac{\omega C}{A}\hat{V}\sin \omega t \qquad (3)$$

and this is of the same form as equation 2, so the given expression for J can be represented by a parallel RC network.

Comparing equations (1) and (3)

$$\omega.\varepsilon_0.\varepsilon_{eff}'.\hat{E} = \frac{\hat{V}}{RA} \qquad (4)$$

and
$$\omega.\varepsilon_0.\varepsilon'.\hat{E} = \frac{\omega C}{A}\hat{V} \qquad (5)$$

Now

$$\hat{E} = \frac{\hat{V}}{d} \quad \text{(where } d = \text{dielectric width)}$$

$\therefore$ from equation (5)

$$\omega\varepsilon_0\varepsilon'\hat{E} = \frac{\omega C}{A}\hat{E}d$$

$$\therefore \quad C = \varepsilon_0\varepsilon'\frac{A}{d}$$

$$\therefore \quad C = \frac{8.85 \times 10^{-.12} \times 1.1 \times 0.01}{0.001}$$

$$= 97.65 \times 10^{-12} \text{ farads}$$

From equation (4)

$$\omega.\varepsilon_0.\varepsilon_{eff}''.\hat{E} = \frac{\hat{E}d}{RA}$$

$$\therefore \quad R = \frac{d}{\omega\varepsilon_0\varepsilon_{eff}''A}$$

$$R = \frac{0.001}{27.12 \times 2\pi \times 10^6 \times 8.85 \times 10^{-12} \times 0.01 \times 0.05}$$

$$= 1.3262 \text{ K}\Omega$$

iii)   Given $P_v = \frac{1}{2}.R_e(J^*.E)$ and $J = j.\omega.\varepsilon_0.E.\varepsilon^*$.

Now

$$E = \frac{\hat{V}}{d}.e^{j\omega t}, \quad \text{let } \hat{E} = \frac{\hat{V}}{d}$$

$$\therefore \quad E = \hat{E}.e^{j\omega t} = \hat{E}.(\cos\omega t + j\sin\omega t)$$

$$J = j.\omega.\varepsilon_0.\hat{E}.(\varepsilon' - j\varepsilon_{eff}'')(\cos\omega t + j\sin\omega t)$$

$$= j.\omega.\varepsilon_0.\hat{E}.(\varepsilon_{eff}''.\cos\omega t - \varepsilon'.\sin\omega t + j(\varepsilon'\cos\omega t + \varepsilon_{eff}''\sin\omega t))$$

but

$$J^* = \omega.\varepsilon_0.\hat{E}.(\varepsilon_{eff}''.\cos\omega t - \varepsilon'.\sin\omega t - j.(\varepsilon'.\cos\omega t + \varepsilon_{eff}''.\sin\omega t))$$

$$\therefore \quad R(J^*.E) = \omega.\varepsilon_0.\hat{E}.\hat{E}.(\varepsilon_{eff}''.\cos^2\omega t - \varepsilon'.\cos\omega t.\sin\omega t$$

$$+ \varepsilon'.\cos\omega t.\sin\omega t + \varepsilon_{eff}''.\sin^2\omega t)$$

$$\tfrac{1}{2}R(J^*.E) = \omega.\varepsilon_0.\frac{\hat{E}^2}{2}.(\cos^2\omega t + \sin^2\omega t).\varepsilon_{eff}''$$

and $\qquad\qquad\qquad P_v = \omega.\varepsilon_0.\varepsilon_{eff}''.E_{RMS}{}^2$ $\qquad\qquad$ QED

In the given case where $f = 27.12\,\text{MHz}$, $\varepsilon_{eff}'' = 0.05$ and the peak field strength $= 1000\,\text{kV/m}$

$$P_v = \omega . \varepsilon_0 . \varepsilon_{eff}'' . \left(\frac{\hat{E}}{\sqrt{2}} \right)^2$$

$$= 27.12 \times 10^6 \times 2\pi \times 8.85 \times 10^{-12} \times 0.05 \left(\frac{1000 \times 10^3}{\sqrt{2}} \right)^2$$

$$P_v = 37.7 \, \text{MW/m}^3$$

DH6

a) Explain why induction heating cannot be used for the direct heating of plastics.

b) Two blocks of wood 20 cm long × 10 cm wide × 3 cm thick to be joined by a 1 mm layer of glue evenly spread over the larger area of the blocks, are placed between the plates of an rf dielectric generator.

Note: The voltage gradient E in an n layer dielectric each of thickness $d_1, d_2 \ldots d_n$ and relative permittivities $\varepsilon_1, \varepsilon_2, \varepsilon_3 \ldots \varepsilon_n$ across which a voltage V is connected is given by

$$E_1 = \frac{V}{d_1 + \dfrac{\varepsilon_1}{\varepsilon_2} d_2 + \ldots \dfrac{\varepsilon_1}{\varepsilon_n} d_n}$$

i) Calculate the time required for the glue to reach its setting temperature of 75 °C if the ambient temperature is 20 °C.

ii) Calculate the temperature of the wood when the glue has just reached a temperature of 75 °C, if conduction losses are neglected.

iii) Specify the power rating of the heater and the value of the applied electrode voltage in order to process 100 of these blocks per hour.

Operating frequency of generator	13.56 MHz
Electrode voltage	11 kV
Loss factor of glue	15.75
Loss factor of wood	0.035
Average specific heat of glue	3.36×10^3 J/kg k
Average specific heat of wood	6.68×10^3 J/kg k
Density of glue	1.3 g/cm^3
Density of wood	0.4 g/cm^3
Relative permittivity of wood	2
Relative permittivity of glue	21
Permittivity of free space	8.85×10^{-12} F/m

(Courtesy of NELP (HND Finals, 1982))

Solution

Power developed in glue/m$^3 = 2\pi f \varepsilon_0 \varepsilon_r \tan \delta . E^2$.

Power required/m^3 to raise the temperature of glue to 75 °C

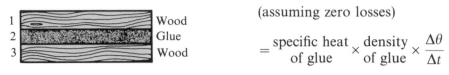

1	Wood
2	Glue
3	Wood

(assuming zero losses)

$$= \frac{\text{specific heat}}{\text{of glue}} \times \frac{\text{density}}{\text{of glue}} \times \frac{\Delta\theta}{\Delta t}$$

Field strength in glue is

$$f_2 = \frac{V}{d_2 + \dfrac{\varepsilon_2}{\varepsilon_1}d_1 \times 2} = \frac{11,000}{0.001 + \frac{21}{2} \times 2 \times 0.03} = 17,460 \text{ V/m}$$

$$2\pi \times 13.56 \times 10^6 \times 8.85 \times 10^{-12} \times 15.75 \times 17,460^2$$
$$= \frac{3.36 \times 10^3 \times 1.3 \times 10^{-3} \times 10^6 (75-20)}{t}$$

or heating time = 66 sec.

$$E_1 = \frac{V}{d_1 + \dfrac{\varepsilon_1}{\varepsilon_2}d_2 + \dfrac{\varepsilon_1}{\varepsilon_2}d_3} = \frac{V}{2d_1} = \frac{11,000}{0.06} = 183 \text{ kV/m}$$

$$2\pi \times 13.5 \times 10^6 \times 8.85 \times 10^{-12} \times 0.035 \times 183^2 \times 10^6$$
$$= \frac{6.68 \times 10^3 \times 0.4 \times 10^{-3} \times 10^6 \, \Delta\theta}{66}$$

$$\Delta\theta = 21.8 \, °C$$

$$\therefore \quad \text{temperature of wood} = 21.8 + 20 = 41.8 \, °C$$

Power required for wood

$$= \frac{6.68 \times 10^3 \times 0.4 \times 10^{-3} \times 10^6 \times 22 \times 10 \times 20 \times 3 \times 2 \times 10^{-6} \times 100}{3600}$$
$$= 1959 \text{ W}$$

Power required for glue

$$= \frac{3.36 \times 10^3 \times 1.3 \times 10^{-3} \times 10^6 \times 55 \times 10 \times 20 \times 0.1 \times 10^{-6} \times 100}{3600}$$
$$= 133 \text{ W}$$

Total power required = 1959 + 133 = 2.1 kW. This rating neglects loading and unloading times since they are not specified.

Now for the glue $k_1 E_1^2 = \dfrac{k_2}{66}$ originally and for the actual work procedure

$$k_1 E_2^2 = \frac{k_2}{36}$$

(since there are 36 seconds per glueing process) where E_2 is
electrode field strength.

We are going to assume that the mechanical presentation of the
work permits continuous usage of the rf generator.

$$\therefore \quad E_2 = \sqrt{\tfrac{66}{36}} \times 17{,}460$$

$$= 23{,}641 \text{ V/m}$$

and required electrode voltage $= 11{,}000 \times \dfrac{23{,}641}{17{,}460}$

$$= 14{,}894 \text{ volts (say } 15\,\text{kV).}$$

DH7

Explain how the length of electrodes in dielectric heating
applications is limited by the frequency of the power source and
show one way of overcoming this problem.

Two blocks of wood each 20×20 cm thick, are to be glued together
using a parallel plate applicator. The plates of the applicator can be
positioned as in Figure 1 or Figure 2.

For the same value of voltage V applied across the electrodes, show
that

a) the setting time for the glue under the conditions of Figure 1 is
    19.4 longer than under conditions of Figure 2.

b) for the same heating time, the temperature rise in the wood for
    the case of Figure 1 is 25 times greater than for the case of
    Figure 2.

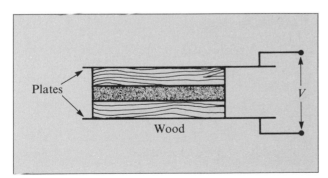

Figure 1

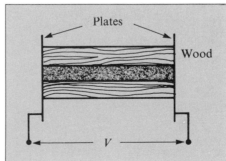

Figure 2

If the loaded Q factor of the applicator is 18 and the unloaded Q
factor for the case of Figure 1 is 150 and for the case of Figure 2 is
250, calculate the applicator efficiency in each case.

The permittivity of the glue used is 22 times larger than the
permittivity of wood and the thickness of the glue layer and heat
losses can be neglected.

(Courtesy of NELP (B.Sc. Finals, 1982))

Solution

In the first part the student would be expected to show how the voltage variation (itself a function of frequency) can lead to a non-uniform field and heating. The use of stubs or multiple feeding along the workpiece length is advocated (see lesson 4, reference 4 and reference 7).

The second part may take the following form:

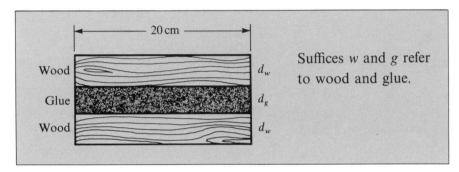

Figure DH7/1

Electrical field strength in wood

$$E_w = \frac{V}{\left[d_w + \frac{\varepsilon_w.d_g}{\varepsilon_g} + d_w \right]}$$

d is thickness, ε is relative permittivity, and

$$E \doteqdot \frac{V}{2d_w}$$

Electrical field strength in glue

$$E_g = \frac{V}{d_g + 2.\frac{\varepsilon_g}{\varepsilon_w}.d_w}$$

$$\doteqdot \frac{V}{2.\varepsilon_g.d_w}$$

For the arrangement in Figure 1.

Power absorbed in glue is given by:

$$2.\pi.f.\varepsilon_0.\varepsilon_g \tan \delta.E_{g_1}{}^2.\left[\frac{M_g}{g_g} \right] = \left[\frac{M_g}{t_1} \right].g_g.\Delta\theta$$

where g_g is density of glue.

For the arrangement in Figure 2.

Power absorbed in glue is given by:

$$2.\pi.f.\varepsilon_0.\varepsilon_g.\tan\delta.E_{g_2}{}^2\left[\frac{M_g}{g_g}\right] = \left[\frac{M_g}{t_2}\right].g_g.\Delta\theta$$

and $\dfrac{E_{g_1}{}^2}{E_{g_2}{}^2} = \dfrac{t_2}{t_1}$; but $E_{g_1} = \dfrac{V.\varepsilon_w}{2.\varepsilon_g.d_w}$ and $E_{g_2} = \dfrac{V}{20}$ V/cm

$$\therefore \quad \frac{E_{g_1}{}^2}{E_{g_2}{}^2} = \frac{V^2.\varepsilon_w{}^2}{4.\varepsilon_g{}^2.d_w{}^2}.\frac{20^2}{V^2} = \frac{t_2}{t_1}$$

or $\quad t_1 = 16.(\tfrac{22}{20})^2.t_2$ because $\dfrac{\varepsilon_g}{\varepsilon_w} = 22$ and $d_w = 2$

and $\quad t_1 = 19.4.t_2.$ \hfill QED

Using the same heating times then

$$\frac{E_{w_1}{}^2}{E_{w_2}{}^2} = \frac{\Delta\theta_1}{\Delta\theta_2} \quad \text{and} \quad E_{w_1} = \frac{V}{2.d_w} \quad \text{and} \quad E_{w_2} = \frac{V}{20}$$

and $\quad \Delta\theta_1 = \Delta\theta_2 \times \dfrac{V^2}{16} \times \dfrac{20^2}{V^2}$

$$= 25.\Delta\theta_2.$$ \hfill QED

For the general case the applicator efficiency $= \left[1 - \dfrac{Q_L}{Q_U}\right] \times 100\%$.

For Figure 1: $\quad \zeta_1 = \left[1 - \dfrac{18}{150}\right] \times 100 = 88\%$

and for Figure 2: $\quad \zeta_2 = \left[1 - \dfrac{18}{250}\right] \times 100 = 92.8\%$

DH8

A radio frequency dryer is to be installed in a paper mill at the end of a conventional drying chamber to level off the moisture content across the paper width. Assuming that the paper enters the radio frequency dryer at 100 °C and neglecting all losses, develop an enthalpy balance for the radio frequency dryer and hence show that if $\varepsilon_{eff}'' = aM + b$, the input and output moisture contents through the radio frequency dryer, M_i and M_f, respectively are related by:

$$(M_f a + b)/(M_i a + b) = \text{constant}$$

You may assume that the power density achieved in the paper is given by:

$$P_m = \frac{\omega . \varepsilon_0}{2} . \varepsilon_{eff}'' . E^2$$

State any assumptions made. In a particular set of running conditions with $M_i = 15\%$, $a = 20$, $b = -1$, the final moisture content M_f was found equal to 8%.

What is the final moisture content for $M_i = 20\%$? Comment on the result.

(Courtesy British National Committee of Electroheat — Summer School 1985)

Solution

Because the temperature of the paper entering the dryer is 100 °C there is no need to consider any sensible heat in the enthalpy balance.

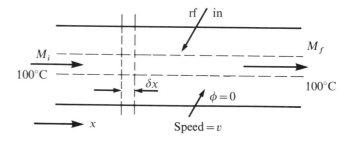

If, in the zone under consideration, the field $E(x, t)$ is maintained constant with time irrespective of the variation in moisture, then the power density is then proportional to ε_{eff}'' and is a function of the moisture M.

Consider the enthalpy balance per kilogram of *dry* paper traversing δx at speed v.

$$\Delta H = h.\delta M \text{ and } \Delta H = \frac{P_m}{\zeta}.\delta t = \frac{\delta x}{v.\zeta} . \frac{\omega.\varepsilon_0}{2} . E^2(x) . \varepsilon_{eff}''(M)$$

latent heat of moisture

and ζ is constant   density

Integrating

$$\int_{M_i}^{M_t} \frac{dM}{\varepsilon_{eff}''(M)} = -\int_{x_1}^{x_2} \frac{\omega.\varepsilon_0}{2} \cdot \frac{1}{v.\zeta} .E^2(x)dx \doteq constant$$

Hence for $\varepsilon_{eff}'' = a.M + b$

$$\ln\left[aM + b \right]_{M_i}^{M_f} = constant$$

and $\dfrac{(aM_f + b)}{(aM_i + b)} = constant \ [= K \ (say)].$ QED

(for a parallel proof see reference 1, pp. 95, 96).

From the given data

$$K = \frac{(0.08 \times 20) - 1}{(0.15 \times 20) - 1} = 0.3$$

For $M_i = 0.2$

$$20M_f = 1 + 0.3 \times 3$$

$$M_f = 0.095$$

The first ratio is $\frac{15}{20}$, ie 0.75 and the second is $\frac{8}{9.5}$, ie 0.84.

Thus the dryness ratio approaches unity and levelling is being achieved.

Note

The power density expression was given for convenience. However, it may form the basis of a proof. Perhaps this would take the form:

Generally

$$J_t = [j.\omega.\varepsilon_0.\varepsilon + \sigma].E \left[= j.\omega\varepsilon_0 \left[\varepsilon - \frac{j.\sigma}{\omega.\varepsilon_0} \right].E \right]$$

If ε' is complex and defined by:

$$\varepsilon^* = \varepsilon' - \frac{j.\sigma}{\omega.\varepsilon_0}$$

Then

$$J_t = j.\omega.\varepsilon_0.\varepsilon'.E$$

However there will be a further direct loss mechanism in this case which will be frequency dependent and of the form $\omega.\varepsilon_0.\varepsilon_r''.E$ where ε_r'' is real.

So that

$$J_t = [j.\omega.\varepsilon_0 + \sigma + \omega.\varepsilon_0\varepsilon_r''].E$$

$$= j.\omega.\varepsilon_0.\varepsilon_{eff}'.E$$

and

$$\varepsilon_{eff}{}' = \varepsilon - j.\left[\frac{\sigma}{\omega.\varepsilon_0} + \varepsilon_r{}''\right]$$

Power dissipated in the paper section will be the real part of $J_t{}^*.E$.

To obtain the power density P_m it is necessary to time average $J_t{}^*.E$ and approximately:

$$P_m = \langle R_e[J_t{}^*.E]\rangle = \langle R_e[j.\omega.\varepsilon_0.\varepsilon_{eff}{}'].E^*.E\rangle$$

$$= \omega t_0\left[\frac{\sigma}{\omega\varepsilon_0} + \varepsilon_r{}''\right].\langle E^*.E\rangle = \omega\varepsilon_0\left[\frac{\sigma}{\omega\varepsilon_0} + \varepsilon_r{}''\right].\frac{1}{2}.E^2$$

putting

$$\varepsilon_{eff}{}'' = \left[\frac{\sigma}{\omega\varepsilon_0} + \varepsilon_r{}''\right] \quad \text{(which is } |J_m[\varepsilon_{eff}{}']|)$$

then

$$P_m = \frac{\omega.\varepsilon_0}{2}.\varepsilon_{eff}{}''.E^2$$

DH9

Explain briefly why standing-waves set up in the applicator of a dielectric heater should be kept to a minimum.

The applicator of an rf paper drying machine operating at 27.12 MHz is to be constructed from lengths of copper tubing having a diameter of 15 mm and spaced with their centres 50 mm apart. The paper to be dried is 4 m wide and a uniform drying rate across the width of the paper is desirable.

Detail an electrode system which will ensure nearly uniform heating across the width of the paper, explaining why the principles on which its design is based. Sketch a schematic diagram of the electrode system and the way it is connected to the dielectric heater. The relative permittivity of paper is unity and the velocity of electromagnetic waves in free space is 3×10^8 m/s.

(Courtesy of NELP (B.Sc. Final, 1977))

Solution
Reference can be made to references 6 (lesson 4) and 48.

Because of standing waves, the power supplied to the material being heated, at the extremities of the applicator will be different from that at the centre and this difference will increase as the length of the applicator approaches half a wavelength. This results in non-uniform heating.

The power input is proportional to V^2 where V is the local potential difference across a pair of electrodes. If it can be arranged that ΣV^2 across the electrodes in the direction of motion of the paper is constant, then uniform heating will result.

Let the peak amplitude of the standing waves on two adjacent pairs of electrodes 1 and 2 be:

$$V_1 = 2V_{\sin}\frac{2\pi y}{\lambda} \quad \text{and} \quad V_2 = 2V\sin\left(\delta + \frac{2\pi y}{\lambda}\right)$$

where V is the peak amplitude of the voltage of the travelling wave.

δ is the phase angle in the standing wave introduced by the type of termination of the line.

$\frac{2\pi y}{\lambda}$ is the phase angle of the wave with y measured from the

termination.

If X is the termination reactance then

$$\tan\delta = \frac{-x}{Z_0}$$

where Z_0 is the characteristic impedance.

Now

$$V_1{}^2 + V_2{}^2 = 4V^2 = \text{constant} \quad \text{if } \delta = \pi/2$$

What is then required for uniform heating is 90° of phase shift to occur between adjacent pairs of electrodes.

This can be achieved by terminating one line with an inductor to give a value of $(-\pi/4)$ for δ and the other by a capacitor to give a

value of $\frac{\pi}{4}$ for δ.

The required value of inductance can be obtained from

$$\omega L = Z_0 = \sqrt{\frac{L_0}{C_0}} = \frac{1}{\pi}\cdot\sqrt{\frac{\mu_0}{\varepsilon_0}}.\ln.(D/r) = 230\,\Omega$$

where r is the radius of the copper tubing, i.e. 7.5 mm and d is the separation distance of 50 mm.

$$\text{At } 27.12\,\text{MHz} \qquad L = 1.35\,\text{mH}$$

similarly $C = \dfrac{1}{\omega Z_0} = 25.5\,\text{pF}.$

If the peak voltage of an inductively terminated line is V_L and V_C is the capacitively terminated line then

$$V_L{}^2 + V_C{}^2 = V_{L_0}{}^2 \sin^2\left(-\frac{\pi}{4} + \frac{2\pi y}{\lambda}\right) + V_{C_0}{}^2.\sin^2\left(\frac{2\pi y}{\lambda} + \frac{\pi}{4}\right)$$

where V_{L_0} and V_{C_0} are the peak voltages on each line.

$$V_L{}^2 + V_C{}^2 = V_{L_0}{}^2 = \text{constant}$$

If V_G is the generator output voltage at the generator end of the line where $y = Y$ and

$$V_G = V_L = V_C$$

then

$$V_C = V_{L_0} \sin\left(\frac{2\pi y}{\lambda} - \frac{\pi}{4}\right) = V_{C_0} \sin\left(\frac{2\pi y}{\lambda} + \frac{\pi}{4}\right)$$

If $Y = \dfrac{n\lambda}{4}$ then $\dfrac{2\pi Y}{\lambda} = \dfrac{n\pi}{2}$ and $V_{L_0} = V_{C_0}$.

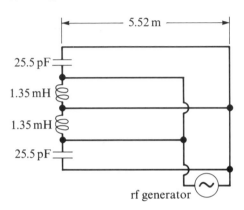

The length of the electrodes must be a multiple of $\lambda/4$. Now

$$\lambda = \frac{c}{f \cdot \sqrt{\varepsilon_r}} = \frac{300}{27.12} = 11.06$$

(since $\varepsilon_r = 1.0$) (see reference 42).

$\lambda/4 = 2.76$ m. This is not wide enough and therefore $2 \times 2.76 = 5.52$ m is then the minimum suitable length for electrode.

An alternative method is to arrange a $\dfrac{\pi}{2}$ phase shift between two adjacent lines. This can be achieved by making one pair $\lambda/4$ longer than the other. The lines are terminated by short circuits as this reduces coupling between the lines and strengthens the electrode system.

As with the previous method the peak voltages on each line must be the same.

The necessary length of line can be obtained from

$$V_G = \left| \hat{V}(\text{long}) \cos \frac{2\pi Y}{\lambda} \right| = \left| \hat{V}(\text{short}) \sin \frac{2\pi Y}{\lambda} \right|$$

If $V_{(\text{long})} = V_{(\text{short})}$

$$\left| \cos \frac{2\pi Y}{\lambda} \right| = \left| \sin \frac{2\pi Y}{\lambda} \right|, \quad \text{i.e.} \quad \frac{2\pi Y}{\lambda} = \frac{\pi}{4}$$

or $Y = (2n-1)\lambda/8; \; n = 1, 2, 3, \dots$.

The nearest length to 4 m is $\dfrac{3\lambda}{8} = 4.14$ m.

This gives the following configuration:

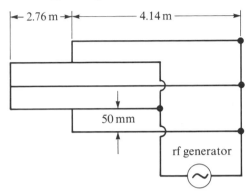

DH10

a) Explain why standing waves in dielectric applicators are undesirable and briefly describe how they may be effectively reduced.

b) A conventional hot-plate press with plates 6 m long, was adopted for radio frequency heating by connecting a 27.12 MHz generator at the mid-point of the press plates. Sketch in fair proportion the resulting standing wave pattern.

c) i) If multiple tuning is carried out by connecting stubs along the plates, calculate the number of stubs required, the distance between the stubs and the inductance of each stub, given the following data:

relative permittivity of wood in the press $=2.4$
power factor of wood $=0.076$
ratio of minimum to maximum voltage appearing on the press $=0.9$
capacitance of press $=700\,\mathrm{pF}$

ii) Show the tuning stubs in position and sketch the voltage distribution along the press electrodes.

(Courtesy of NELP (HND in Elec & El. Eng. 1978))

Solution

a) see DH9

b) Wavelength $\lambda = \dfrac{v}{f\sqrt{\varepsilon_r}} = \dfrac{3\times 10^8}{27.12\times 10^6 \times 2.4} = 7.14\,\mathrm{m}$

and $\lambda/4 = \dfrac{7.14}{4} = 1.78\,\mathrm{m}$, giving:

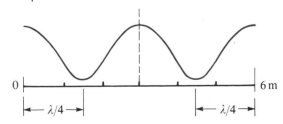

c) i) $\quad E = \hat{E}\cos\left(\dfrac{360}{7.14}\dfrac{d}{2}\right)$ where d = spacing between stubs

$$\text{or } \dfrac{360d}{2 \times 7.14} = \cos^{-1} 0.9 = 25.8$$

$$\text{or } d = \dfrac{25.8 \times 2 \times 7.14}{360} = 1.02\,\text{m}$$

$\therefore$ 6 tuning stubs spaced 1 m apart.

$$L = \dfrac{6}{4\pi^2 \times 27.12^2 \times 10^{12} \times 700 \times 10^{-12}} = 0.295\,\text{H}$$

c) ii)

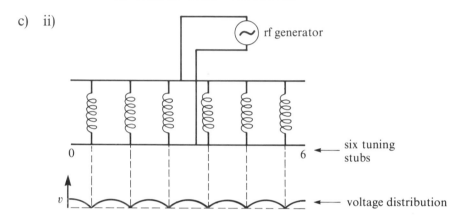

DH11

Briefly compare microwave with radio frequency dielectric heating.

A batch of six plastic pellets is preheated to 85 °C for 30 sec. in preparation for moulding in a parallel plate applicator supplied from a 27.12 MHz dielectric heater. Each pellet weighs 25 g and is of cylindrical shape having a diameter 6 cm and height of 1 cm. The plates of the applicator, which are in contact with the flat surface of the pellets, are 20 cm long and 13 cm wide. Assuming no heat losses from the plates, for an ambient temperature of 20 °C calculate:

i)   the power requirements

ii)   the equivalent parallel capacitance and resistance of the loaded applicator

iii)   the voltage developed across the electrodes

iv)   the applicator efficiency, if the unloaded Q factor of the applicator is 300.

Permittivity of free space 8.85×10^{-12} F/m
For the pellet
Specific heat 1592 J/kgK
Loss factor 0.06
Relative permittivity 2.5

(Courtesy of NELP (B.Sc. Finals, 1983))

Solution

The student would be expected to describe the frequency difference, rf produces mainly conduction heating with higher fields. In turn this gives a propensity to breakdown conditions. The mechanism with microwave is dipolar. Lower electricity fields are possible (hence 'safer') and larger power densities in the work are possible.

i) power requirements $= \dfrac{1592 \times 25 \times 6 \times 10^{-3}(85-20)}{30} = 517.4\,\text{W}$

for the batch.

ii) area of plate occupied by pellets $= 6\pi[3 \times 10^{-2}]^2$

$$= 1.696 \times 10^{-2}\,\text{m}^2$$

unoccupied area of plates $= 20 \times 13 \times 10^{-4} - 1.696 \times 10^{-2}$

$$= 9.04 \times 10^{-3}\,\text{m}^2$$

Capacitance of loaded applicator

$$= \frac{8.85 \times 10^{-12}}{1 \times 10^{-2}}[9.04 \times 10^{-3} + 1.696 \times 2.5 \times 10^{-2}]$$

$$= 45.52\,\text{pF}$$

Capacitance of pellets alone

$$= \frac{8.85 \times 10^{-12}}{1 \times 10^{-2}} \times 1.696 \times 2.5 \times 10^{-2} = 37.52\,\text{pF}$$

$$R_a = \frac{1}{\omega C_a \tan \delta} = \frac{2.5}{2\pi \times 27.12 \times 10^6 \times 0.06 \times 37.52 \times 10^{-12}}$$

$$= 6.52\,\text{k}\Omega$$

[because $\varepsilon_r \tan \delta = 0.06$].

iii) Volume of pellets $= 6[\pi \times 3^2 \times 1] \times 10^{-6}\,\text{m}^3$.

If E is the electric field, then

$$517 = 2\pi \times 27.12 \times 10^6 \times 8.85 \times 10^{-12} \times 0.06 \times E^2 \times 6 \times \pi \times 9 \times 10^{-6}$$

$$= 15{,}350.E^2 \times 10^{-12} \quad \text{or} \quad E = 0.1835 \times 10^6\,\text{Vm}^{-1}$$

and the voltage across electrodes

$$V = E \times d = 0.1835 \times 10^6 \times 1 \times 10^{-2} = 1.83\,\text{kV}$$

iv)
$$V = \sqrt{\frac{PQ_L}{WC_t}} \quad \text{or} \quad Q = \frac{V^2 \omega c_t}{P}$$

or

$$Q_L = \frac{(1.83 \times 10^3)^2 \times 2\pi \times 27.12 \times 10^6 \times 45.52 \times 10^{-12}}{517.4} = 50$$

or from

$$\omega C_p R_p = 2\pi \times 27.12 \times 10^6 \times 45.52 \times 6.52 \times 10^3 \times 10^{-12}$$

$$= 50$$

$$\eta = [1 - \tfrac{50}{300}].100 = 83.3\%$$

DH12

A material of relative complex permittivity $(2.5 - j0.03)$ is passed between two electrodes which have a 27 MHz, 3 kV potential applied between them. The material is carried on a flat metal conveyor which forms the lower electrode and the upper electrode is a flat plate 0.3 m wide and 2 m long. The material is 0.005 m thick and the air gap between the material and the upper electrode is 0.008 m.

a) Calculate the speed at which the conveyor must move if the material is to be heated from 20 °C to 90 °C on its passage through the electrodes.

b) Sketch the voltage distribution along the length of the electrode if the generator is connected between one end of the top electrode and the conveyor.

c) If the material is to be heated by passing it through a four pass serpentine applicator at the same speed as in (a), the applicator being supplied from a 2 kW microwave generator, determine if sufficient power will be extracted from the generator for the material to reach a temperature of 90 °C.

Specific heat of material $= 500 \, \mathrm{J \, kg^{-1} \, K^{-1}}$
Density of material $7000 \, \mathrm{kg/m^3}$
Velocity of light $3 \times 10^8 \, \mathrm{m \, s^{-1}}$
Permittivity of free space $8.85 \times 10^{-12} \, \mathrm{F/m}$
Attenuation of waveguide and material 25.3×10^{-3} nepers/m.

(*Courtesy Electroheat Teaching Workshops British National Committee of Electroheat 1979–85*)

Solution

a) Field strength across material $= \dfrac{3000}{0.005 + 2.5 \times 0.008}$

$$= 120 \, \mathrm{kVm^{-1}}.$$

Power developed in material

$$= 2\pi \times 27 \times 10^6 \times 8.85 \times 10^{-12} \times 0.03 \times 120^2 \times 10^6$$

$$= 648.6 \, \mathrm{kWm^{-3}}$$

Heat required to raise the material to 90 °C

$$= 7000 \times 500(90 - 20) = 245,000 \, \mathrm{kJm^{-3}}$$

Time required to move through the electrodes

$$= \frac{245{,}000}{648.6} = 378 \text{ s}$$

$\therefore$ speed of conveyor $= 0.53 \text{ cm s}^{-1}$.

b) Wavelength $\lambda = \dfrac{3 \times 10^8}{27 \times 10^6 \sqrt{2.5}} = 7 \text{ m}$.

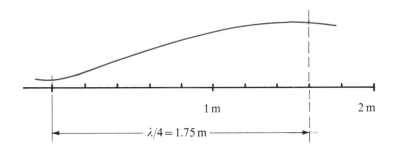

c) Volume of material $= 2 \times 0.3 \times 0.005 = 3 \times 10^{-3} \text{ m}^3$

power required $= 648.6 \times 3 \times 10^{-3} = 1.95 \text{ kW}$

attenuation $= 25.3 \times 10^{-3}$ nepers m^{-1} $= 0.22$ db m^{-1}
total length of waveguide $= 4 \times 0.3 = 1.2$ m (each pass is across width of conveyor)

total attenuation $= 1.2 \times 0.22 = 0.264$ db

If P is the ratio of power transmitted to power absorbed,

$$0.264 = 10 \log_{10} P \text{ or } P = 1.06$$

$\therefore$ only 6% of the available power will be absorbed by the material which is insufficient to raise it to 90 °C since power required is 1.95 kW.

DH13

a) Develop an expression for the electric field strength developed across a material placed within a parallel plate applicator in the presence of a uniform airgap above the material.

b) A block of material 25 cm × 25 cm × 3 cm is heated from a temperature of 15 °C to 150 °C by a 13.56 MHz parallel plate applicator. The heater has a uniform air-gap of thickness 3 mm between the surface of the load and its upper electrode and the heating time is 1145 s.

On the assumptions that the loss factor remains constant, the heat losses can be neglected and the applicator voltage is a constant 1 kV, calculate:

i) the relative permittivity of the material,

ii) the size of the air-gap required to reduce the heating time to 800 s.

For the material:

$$loss\ factor = 0.31$$

$$specific\ heat = 950\ \mathrm{J\,kg^{-1}\,K^{-1}}$$

$$density = 1400\ \mathrm{kg\,m^{-3}}$$

$$permittivity\ of\ air = 8.85 \times 10^{-12}\ \mathrm{Fm^{-1}}$$

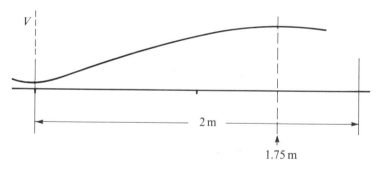

(*Courtesy Electroheat Teaching Workshops British National Committee of Electroheat 1979–85*)

Solution

a) The student should give the derivation of the expression:

$$E\ material = \frac{Applicator\ voltage}{material\ thickness + \varepsilon_{r_m}.\ air\ gap\ thickness}$$

b) i) Heat required $= 1.4 \times 10^3 . 950 . (150 - 15) = 180\ \mathrm{MJm^{-3}}$, and

$$\left[\frac{180}{heat\ developed}\right] = 1145$$

$$\therefore\quad heat\ developed = 157\ \mathrm{MJm^{-3}}$$

Again, heat developed $= 2\pi \times 13.56 \times 10^6 \times 8.85 \times 10^{-12} \times 0.31 \times E^2$, where E is the electric field strength in $V\,m^{-1}$.

$$\therefore \quad E^2 = \frac{157 \times 10^3}{2\pi \times 13.56 \times 10^6 \times 8.85 \times 10^{-12} \times 0.31} = 6.72 \times 10^8$$

$$E = 2.59 \times 10^4 = 25.9 \, kV\,m^{-1}$$

$$25.9 \times 10^3 = \frac{1000}{0.03 + \varepsilon_r 0.003}$$

$$\therefore \quad \varepsilon_r = \frac{1 - 25.9 \times 0.03}{25.9 \times 0.003} = 2.87$$

where ε_r is the required *relative* permittivity.

ii)
$$\frac{180 \times 10^6}{Heat} = 800$$

$$Heat = 225 \, kW m^{-3}$$

and
$$\frac{225}{157} = \frac{E_m{}^2}{25.9^3}$$

giving
$$E_m = 31 \, kV m^{-3}$$

and
$$31 \times 10^3 = \frac{1000}{0.03 + 2.87 \times t}$$

where t is the thickness of the air gap, or

$$t = \frac{1 - 31 \times 0.03}{31 \times 2.87} = 0.8 \, mm$$

DH14

A radio frequency (rf) power source is to be used to cure PVC-treated, heavy-duty, woven conveyor belting, at the rate of 15,250 kg per 24 hours. In order to obtain some data which will enable the prediction of the performance of an electrode system to be used for this application, the circuit of Fig. DH14/1 was set up and the following tests carried out.

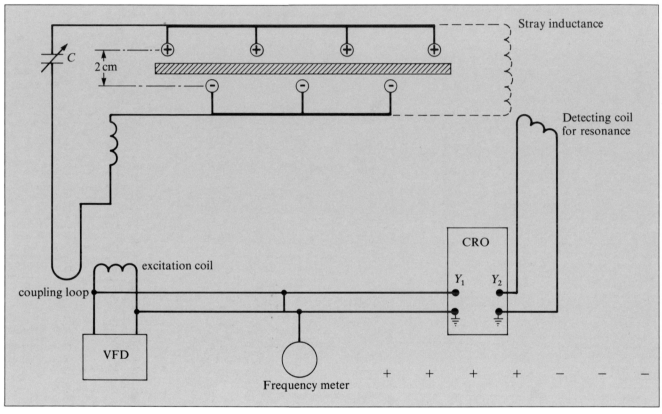

Figure DH14/1

The electrode system was excited by the excitation coil and capacitor C was adjusted to resonate the applicator system at 27 MHz with the applicator unloaded.

A complete resonance curve was then obtained, first with the applicator unloaded, secondly with the applicator loaded with the uncured belting and finally with the applicator loaded with cured belting. The respective resonance curves are shown in Figure DH14/2(a), (b) and (c), respectively. The measured capacitance of the capacitor C at resonance was 90 pF and that of the loaded applicator was 112 pF. If the average specific heat of the belting is 1257 J/kg°C, the belting thickness is 1 cm, the area of belting presented to the electrodes is 1 m^2 and a temperature rise of 144 °C is required to cure it, use the information given and the above test results to estimate:

a)   the required minimum power output of the rf power source,

b)   the predicted value of voltage which will be developed across the electrodes when the applicator is loaded and connected to the rf power source at the beginning and at the end of the heating period,

c)   the maximum possible predicted power input to the belting in the uncured state.

(Courtesy of NELP (B.Sc. Finals, 1978))

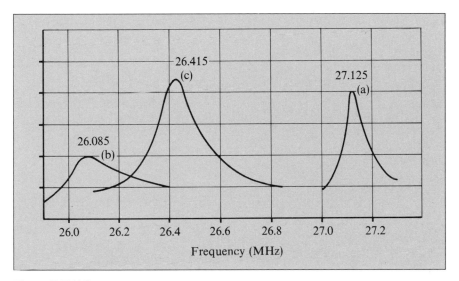

Figure DH14/2

Solution

a)   From graph DH14/2a Q of unloaded applicator

$$Q_0 = \frac{f_0}{f_1 - f_2} = \frac{27.125}{27.1625 - 27.099} = 414$$

where f_1 and f_2 are at the 3 dB points and at the

frequency where $\dfrac{1}{\sqrt{2}} \times$ (Response at f_0) occurs.

From graph DH14/2(c) Q of applicator loaded with cured material

$$Q_{L_1} = \frac{26.415}{26.480 - 26.362} = 224$$

From graph DH14/2b Q of applicator with uncured material

$$Q_{L_2} = \frac{26.085}{26.220 - 26.010} = 124$$

$$\eta = 1 - \frac{Q_L}{Q_0}$$

for uncured belting

$$\eta = 1 - \frac{124}{414} = 0.7$$

for cured belting

$$\eta = 1 - \frac{224}{414} = 0.46$$

($\eta =$ the fraction of power delivered to the load).

Power required by belting

$$= \frac{15{,}250 \times 1257 \times 144}{24 \times 3600} = 32\,\text{kW}$$

Minimum power output of rf power source $= \dfrac{32}{0.54} = 59\,\text{kW}$.

b) $V = \sqrt{\dfrac{PQ}{\omega C}}$ where C is the series combination of 90 pF and 112 pF, thus $C = 50\,\text{pF}$

$$\therefore \quad V = \sqrt{\frac{59 \times 10^3 \times 124 \times 10^{12}}{2\pi \times 27.12 \times 10^6 \times 50}} = 29.3\,\text{kV}$$

for the uncured belting, appearing across C.

Similarly for the cured condition $V = 39.38\,\text{kV}$.

Voltage developed across electrodes when loaded with uncured material

$$= \frac{V X_{C1}}{X_{C_1} + X_{C_2}} = 29.55 \times \frac{52.3}{52.3 + 65.2} = 13.15\,\text{kV}$$

Voltage appearing across electrodes when loaded with material is

$$39.72 \times \frac{52.3}{52.3 + 65.2} = 17.68\,\text{kV}$$

c) $\tan\delta = \dfrac{1}{Q} = \dfrac{1}{124} = 0.0080645$

$$E_r = \left[\frac{f_0}{f}\right]^2 = \frac{27.125}{26.0850} = 1.0813$$

$$E_r \tan\delta = 0.0087$$

Power input to belting $= kE^2f\varepsilon_r\tan\delta$

$$= 0.556 \times 10^{-13}\left(\frac{13.15}{2}\right)^2 \times 27.12 \times 10^6 \times 0.0051$$

$$= 5671 \, kW/m^3$$

or 56.7 kW.

DH15

Explain briefly why standing waves are undesirable with long applicators.

A sheet of wood veneer is to be glued to a pine block. Glue is spread evenly on the pine block and the assembly of veneer, glue and pine block is placed between the plates of an rf generator operating at 13.56 MHz. The surface area of each applicator plate is 1 m² and the parameters of the materials involved are given in Table 1. If the output voltage from the generator is 3 kV and the maximum power output is 5 kW calculate:

a)   The inductance required to tune the loaded applicator to the generator frequency,

b)   The turns ratio of a matching transformer to enable the maximum power to be available to the load,

c)   The power developed in the glue line.

Table 1

Material	Thickness (mm)	Dielectric Constant	Loss Factor
Veneer	0.3	4	0.05
Glue	0.1	15	5
Pine block	25	4	0.05

(*Courtesy of NELP B.Sc. 1986*)

Solution

A standing wave will infer a standing maximum and minimum condition of temperature corresponding to the field pattern. Where the length of an applicator approaches the wave-length (or half a wave length), clearly uneven heating will occur. Quite arbitrarily a practical length equivalent to $\lambda/10$ seems in practice to be acceptable.

Giving the subscripts 1, 2 and 3 to Veneer, Glue and Pine-block respectively, then the following equivalent circuits arise:

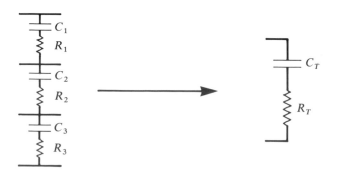

and assuming negligible resistance in the tuning inductance the circuit arrangement becomes:

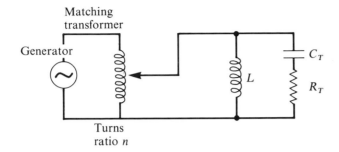

Now

$$C_1 = \frac{\varepsilon_0.\varepsilon_{r1}.A}{d_1} \qquad c_2 = \frac{\varepsilon_0.\varepsilon_{r2}.A}{d_2} \qquad c_3 = \frac{\varepsilon_0.\varepsilon_{r3}.A}{d_3}$$

$$= \frac{8.85 \times 10^{-12} \times 4 \times 1}{0.3 \times 10^{-3}} \qquad = \frac{8.85 \times 10^{-12} \times 15 \times 1}{0.1 \times 10^{-3}} \qquad = \frac{8.85 \times 10^{-12} \times 4 \times 1}{2.5 \times 10^{-3}}$$

$$= 0.118 \,\mu F \qquad\qquad = 1.328 \,\mu F \qquad\qquad = 1.416 \times 10^{-3} \,\mu F$$

and

$$C_T = \frac{0.118 \times 1.328 \times 1.416 \times 10^{-3}}{[0.118 \times 1.328 + 0.118 \times 1.416 \times 10^{-3} + 1.416 \times 10^{-3} \times 1.328]}$$

$$= 1.398 \times 10^{-3} \,\mu F$$

The inductance L required to tune the load and applicator is given by:

$$L = \frac{1}{\omega^2.C_T} = \frac{1}{4 \times \pi^2 \times 13.56^2 \times 10^{12} \times 1398 \times 10^{-12}} \text{ (approximately)}$$

$$= 0.0985 \,\mu H$$

Again $R_n = \frac{1}{\omega.C}.\tan\delta$ (for series representation)

and

$$\tan\delta_1 = \frac{0.05}{4}; \quad \tan\delta_2 = \frac{5}{15}; \quad \tan\delta_3 = \frac{0.05}{4}$$

So that

$$R_1 = \frac{1}{\omega.c_1}.\frac{0.05}{4}$$

$$= \frac{0.05}{13.56} \times 10^6 \times 2 \times \pi \times 0.118 \times 10^{-6} \times 4$$

$$= 1.24 \times 10^{-3} \text{ ohms}$$

Similarly,

$$R_2 = 2.94 \times 10^{-3} \text{ ohms}$$

and

$$R_3 = 0.1036 \text{ ohms}$$

and

$$R_T = 0.108 \text{ ohms}$$

Impedance at resonance $\doteqdot \dfrac{L}{C_T . R_T}$

$$= \frac{0.0985 . 10^{-6}}{1398 . 10^{-12} . 0.108}$$

$$= 652 \text{ ohms}$$

The resistance seen by the generator to give full output is

$$\frac{3000^2}{5000} = 1800 \text{ ohms}$$

Thus the turns ratio of the matching transformer n

$$= \sqrt{\frac{1800}{652}} = 1.66$$

and the voltage across the applicator $= \dfrac{3000}{1.66}$

$$= 1807 \text{ volts}$$

Field strength across the glue is given by:

$$E_2 = \frac{v}{\left[d_2 + \dfrac{\varepsilon_2}{\varepsilon_1} . d_1 + \dfrac{\varepsilon_2}{\varepsilon_3} . d_3 \right]}$$

$$= \frac{1807}{\left[0.1 + \dfrac{15}{4}(0.3 + 25) \right] . 10^{-3}}$$

$$= 19.13 \text{ kV/m}$$

Power developed in glue

$$= 2.\pi.f.\varepsilon_0.\varepsilon_r.\tan\delta.E^2 \times \text{volume}$$

$$= 2 \times \pi \times 13.56 \times 10^6 \times 8.85 \times 10^{-12} \times 5 \times 19.13^2 \times 10^6 \times 0.1 \times 10^{-3} \times 1$$

$$= 138 \text{ watts}$$

Metal melting (resistance and induction)

CHAPTER 6

6.1. Background to the teaching

At this point, having covered direct, indirect and induction heating of conductors and dielectric heating it is now possible to link these various mechanisms together to consider metal melting. Metal melting using arc and discharge mechanisms will be considered later so that the family of melting furnaces now discussed will lie within those categories which include coreless, channel and associated crucible induction furnaces, resistance crucible furnaces and specific direct resistance processes associated with consumable electrodes.

It has been found convenient to treat metal melting merely as an extension of the various principal mechanisms. This has been the practice adopted by the author in his research and development work and more latterly with his colleagues in teaching. This was also the procedure followed by Paschkis and Persson[49] and much earlier by Burch and Davis[50]. Robiette broke away from this tradition and his book on melting practice[51] remains today an excellent, albeit mainly descriptive treatment. Alas like many such books there is a need for up-dating. Robiette hardly mentions the 'solid-state' medium frequency supply (now the norm), there is no reference to the integral replaceable crucible induction furnace now numerically exceeding its larger relatives used for tonnage applications and the vertical channel furnace receives no mention. An improved and more detailed treatment is given by Harrison[6] but it could be that this work is too detailed for other than practising engineers.

In this present case several examples are drawn together and where appropriate attention is drawn to specialised references. Some of these examples are not of the half-hour examination type, but are included to provide a source for a tutorial assignment.

6.2. The worked examples

MM1

Describe a simple electroslag remelting plant. For what reason would such a plant be used?

Steel billets 2 m long and 100 mm in diameter are to be melted into an electroslag refining unit to form an ingot of approximately 250 mm in diameter. The refined ingot is to weigh approximately 3 tonnes. A melt rate of 120 kg/h has been determined as a necessary condition for operation. Find the number of billets per ingot, determine the mould size and indicate briefly some aspects of its design, and finally suggest a suitable dc power rating. What would be the implications of using an ac supply?

Take the density of the steel as 7850 kg/m^3, the maximum metal and slag temperature as 2000 K when the heat contents of molten metal and slag (based on calcium fluoride) above ambient temperature of 15 °C are 1480 MJ/t and 2450 MJ/t respectively. Use a slag:metal weight ratio of 1:20. The emissivity of the slag is 0.96 and the Stefan-Boltzmann constant is 5.67×10^{-8} W m^{-2} K^{-4}.

Take cooling water temperature as 60 °C and its heat transfer coefficient (conductivity) as 2000 W/m^{2}K and that of the copper available as 375 m^{2}K/W and wall thickness 3 cm. The slag thermal conductivity is 1.35 m^{2}K/W and that of steel 50,000 m^{2}K/W.

(The author)

Solution
The student would simply be expected to describe a single consumable electrode system (see reference 18). The reasons for using the process are to do with improving steel quality particularly the reduction of porosity and improvement of cleanliness (again see pp. 8–9, reference 18). Other arrangements are described in reference 52.

The example deliberately picks a slow melting rate (with therefore low efficiency). This melting rate is associated with high quality steels particularly for ball bearing quality.

dc is preferred for large ingots but interestingly the use of ac aids desulphurisation with appropriate slags.

The corollary to the example on the use of ac would lead a student to either comment on the chemistry or the need for no power factor compensation with dc systems. Normally these systems run with relatively low voltages ($\ngtr$ 60 volts for high quality steels) and high currents giving rise to high reactance in the secondary circuit.

The example following ignores losses in the base plate of the mould and in the secondary circuit including any electrode clamps. A good student noting the number of billets/ingot might wish to observe that electrode changing perhaps using a dual head, or a clamp slip to permit the addition of a new billet length is necessary.

The ingot length L is given by:

Ingot volume × density = 3000 (the specified weight of refined ingot).

$$\frac{\pi \times 0.25^2}{4} \times L \times 7850 = 3000$$

Giving $\qquad L = 7.79$ metres.

$$\text{Number of billets/ingot} = \frac{0.25^2 \times 7.79}{0.100^2 \times 2}$$

$$= 24.34 \quad \text{say 25 billets}$$

The mould size needs to allow for shrinkage after solidification.

Mould size is given by

$$\frac{\pi D_m{}^2 L_m}{4} = \frac{\pi 0.25^2}{4} \times 7.79 + \text{shrinkage volume (say 8\%)}$$

mould diameter is to be 270 mm (say)

and mould length 8.41 m (say).

Again the mould length needs to accommodate the slag. A total slag height of 3 cm will be assumed and with a further allowance of 10 cm to avoid electrode/slag splash a total mould length of 8.6 m approx. is suggested.

Hence use a mould 8.6 m high by 0.27 m internal diameter

The melting rate of 120 kg/h infers a melting time of $\frac{3000}{120}$, ie 25 hours.

The melting energy E required to melt 1 t of steel with 0.05 t of slag is:

$$E = 1480 + 0.05 \times 2450$$

$$= 1602 \text{ MJ}$$

$$= 445 \text{ kWh}$$

Over 25 hours this requires a power input of $\frac{445}{25} = 17.8$ kW. It is now necessary to determine the associated losses.

The exposed surface area of the bath is A_b

$$A_b = \frac{\pi \times 0.27^2}{4} - \frac{\pi \times 0.1^2}{4} = 0.049 \text{ m}^2$$

Then the radiated power loss P_r is given by:

$$P_r = 0.96 \times 5.67 \times 10^{-8} \times 0.049 \times [2000^4 - (273 + 15)^4] \times 10^{-3}$$

$$= 42.6 \, \text{kW}$$

Again it is assumed a water cooled mould is employed.

We now need to determine the losses due essentially to the mould cooling mechanism. First with a copper crucible its area in contact with the solidifying ingot will be $\pi \times 0.27 \times 7.79 = 6.61 \, \text{m}^2$.

As a pessimistic view it will be assumed the ingot remains molten to the base-plate throughout the melting cycle.

The heat transfer to the cooling water will be determined from a heat transfer coefficient α where

$$\frac{1}{\alpha} = \frac{1}{\text{water thermal conductivity}} + \frac{\text{crucible wall thickness}}{\text{crucible thermal conductivity}}$$

$$+ \frac{\text{slag thickness}}{\text{slag thermal conductivity}} + \frac{\text{thickness of molten metal}}{\text{steel thermal conductivity}}$$

$$= \frac{1}{2000} + \frac{0.03}{375} + \frac{0.03}{1.35} + \frac{6.61}{50,000}$$

the last term is very much a guess!

$$\therefore \quad \frac{1}{\alpha} = 5.0 \times 10^{-4} + 8 \times 10^{-5} + 2.22 \times 10^{-2} + 1.322 \times 10^{-4}$$

$$= 2.29 \times 10^{-2}$$

$$\therefore \quad \alpha \doteqdot 43.64$$

$\therefore$ losses to the water are $43.64 \times 6.61 \times 1712.0 \times 10^{-3} = 493.8 \, \text{kW}$.

Thus the total power required is $493.8 + 42.6 + 17.8 = 554.24 \, \text{kW}$.

MM2

Describe briefly the possible electrical options open in providing new molten metal to a zinc galvanising line.

Almost pure zinc is to be used in a galvanising line and it is known that the heat content of the metal as determined experimentally is:

100	200	300	400	600	800 °C
12	23	34	46	102	132 kWh/t referred to 0 °C

The metal melts at around 415 °C and the metal is to be delivered to a galvanising tank at 550 °C. The metal at 550 °C with its oxide exhibits an emissivity of 0.53 [Stefan-Boltzmann constant $= 5.67.10^{-8} \, \text{J/m}^2.\text{s.K}$].

It is required to produce 100 kg of metal at 550 °C in one hour from 20.°C. A standard cast iron crucible weighing 60 kg of specific heat 0.5 kJ/kg K is to be used, which allows a molten metal surface area of 0.21 m². Determine the required power input to the crucible–metal combination.

The crucible manufacturer estimates the standing loss from the crucible shell at 550 °C to be 2.0 kW.

Would the power input be sufficient to deliver 50 kg of metal continuously starting from a full furnace at 550 °C?

(The author)

Solution

There are two furnace types based on either indirect resistance (element) or induction heating. Both furnace types in turn will permit the use of either refractory or iron/steel crucibles. Cast iron crucibles tend to be preferred for zinc and its alloys and the student with some metallurgical knowledge might refer to the use of high alumina, zirconia or silica refractories.

If the duty cycle is intermittent, ie charging once every two or three shifts or so from cold or 'topping up' over one shift in three then a steel crucible would be preferred.

The unwary student may refer to the use of immersion heaters!!

The table is given to avoid the notorious confusion often arising in using specific heats at various temperatures for metals. However, the student would be expected to state what use of the table is made. The jump from 400 to 600 °C includes the change of state and the ensuing latent heat. However, up to 400 °C the kWh/t.K is reasonably linear at 11 kWh/t.K. Specific heats of most metals increase from the solid to liquid state so the student could assume linear heat content change within a given state.

Thus the heat content at 550 °C may be derived from

$$H_{550} - 102 - 50 \times \frac{30}{200}$$

$$= 94.5 \, \text{kWh/t and referred to } 20\,°\text{C, say } 92 \, \text{kWh/t}$$

Thus the heat required to heat the metal to 550 °C

$$= \frac{92}{1000} \times 100 = 9.2 \, \text{kWh}$$

Heat required to heat the cast iron crucible

$$= \frac{60 \times 0.5 \times (550 - 20)}{3600}$$

$$= 4.42 \, \text{kWh}$$

The heat loss from the metal surface at $550\,^\circ$C

$$\doteqdot 0.53 \times 5.67 \times 10^{-8} \times 823^4 \times 0.21$$

$$= 2.9\,\text{kW}$$

(assume over the start-up period heat loss is 1.5 kWh).

The standing loss from the crucible at $550\,^\circ$C is 2.0 kW, again assume over the start up period this is 1.0 kWh.

Thus the total heat required

$$= 9.2 + 4.4 + 1.5 + 1.0 = 16\,\text{kWh}$$

And the power required

$$= 16\,\text{kW}$$

since the melting time is one hour.

In practice dependent on the furnace type an allowance for electrical losses would be required. The question has not requested the student to pursue this point.

The thermal capacity of 50 kg of metal	$= \frac{92}{1000} \times 50$
	$= 4.6\,\text{kWh}$
The standing loss from the crucible	$= 2.0\,\text{kWh}$
The heat loss per hour from the metal surface	$= 2.9\,\text{kWh}$
The heat to supply 50 kg per hour	$= 9.5\,\text{kWh}$

Viz: a power input of 9.5 kW.

Thus if a furnace is designed to provide a power input of 16 kW to the crucible/metal combination it will meet both operational requirements.

MM3

For a coreless induction furnace with an assumed cylindrical melt, show that applied power P is proportional to the square root of applied coil voltage frequency times the square of the effective field strength (or $P \alpha f^{1/2}.H^2$).

Assuming the melt is a 'perfect' fluid, show that metal velocity is proportional to field strength by equating centrifugal force to electromagnetic force or otherwise.

A given furnace fed at 150 Hz melts iron to a temperature of 1550°C (thus near to a 'perfect' fluid). The stir is judged to be too fierce for superheating purposes. What frequency is required to reduce the stirring velocity to one third that of the original design at 1550°C?

(The author)

Solution

$$P = I^2.R \qquad\qquad R = \frac{\rho \pi D}{\delta l}$$

$$R \alpha \frac{1}{\delta} \text{ and} \qquad\qquad \delta = \frac{k}{f}$$

$$R \alpha f$$

again $H \alpha I$ so that $P \alpha f^{1/2}.H^2$.   QED

Centrifugal force of vortex is proportional to (velocity)^2. The velocity is tangential and thus that measured at melt surface. Electromagnetic force is proportional to (coil current)^2, ie H^2

$$\therefore \quad \text{metal velocity } \alpha H$$

Stirring velocity $\alpha \dfrac{P^{1/2}}{f^{1/2}}$ power applied remains unchanged

$$\frac{V_1}{V_2} = \left[\frac{f_2}{f_1}\right]^{1/4}$$

$$\text{ie } f_2 = \left[\frac{V_1}{V_2}\right]^4.150 = [3]^4.150 = 12,150 \text{ Hz}$$

$$= 12 \text{ k Hz (say)}$$

MM4

The magnetic field, B, of a coreless induction furnace is poloidal with components B_r and B_z in cylindrical coordinates and is related to its vector potential A by $B = \text{curl } A$. The current density J, electric field E and potential A are all azimuthal vectors with components J_θ, E_θ and A_θ. It can also be assumed throughout that $\partial/\partial\theta = 0$.

Deduce the components of the force $J \times B$ and assuming that the component A_θ is periodic with variations in the form $A_\theta = a\cos(\omega t + \phi)$ where a and ϕ are functions of r and z, show that the mean stirring force F is given by

$$F = (J \times B)_{\text{mean}} = -(\omega\sigma a^2/2)\nabla\phi$$

where σ is the melt conductivity given from $J = \sigma E$ and $E = -\partial A/\partial t$. Hence show that the expression for the mean stirring force density is

$$S = |\text{curl } F| = \omega\sigma a\left(\frac{\partial a}{\partial z}\frac{\partial\phi}{\partial z} - \frac{\partial a}{\partial z}\frac{\partial\phi}{\partial r}\right)$$

(*Electroheat Tutorials — Cambridge University*)

Solution

Given $A = A_\theta = a\cos(\omega t + \phi)$, also assume $\dfrac{\partial}{\partial\theta} = 0$.

Cylindrical coordinates become for magnetic field poloidal B_r and B_z.

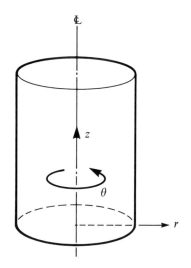

The current is azimuthal represented by J_θ.

Hence the $J \times B$ vector has the following components:

$$J \times B = \begin{vmatrix} a_r & a_\theta & a \\ J_r & J_\theta & J_z \\ B_r & B_\theta & B_z \end{vmatrix} = \begin{vmatrix} a_r & a_\theta & a_z \\ 0 & J_\theta & 0 \\ B_r & 0 & B_z \end{vmatrix}$$

$$= a_r J_\theta B_z - a_z J_\theta B_r \tag{1}$$

126

Now $B = \nabla \times A$ in cylindrical coordinates. Then

$$\nabla \times A = \frac{1}{r} \cdot \begin{vmatrix} a_\theta & ra_\theta & a_z \\ \dfrac{\partial}{\partial r} & 0 & \dfrac{\partial}{\partial z} \\ A_r & rA_\theta & A_z \end{vmatrix} = \frac{-a_r \, \partial A_\theta r}{r \, \partial z} + a_\theta \cdot \left(\frac{\partial A_r}{\partial z} - \frac{\partial A_z}{\partial r} \right)$$

$$= a_z \cdot \frac{1}{r} \cdot \frac{\partial}{\partial r}(A_\theta \cdot r)$$

But this is equal to B or $a_r B_r + a_z B_z$.

Equating coefficients yields

$$B_r = \frac{1}{z} \cdot \frac{\partial}{\partial z}(A_\theta \cdot r) \text{ and } B_z = \frac{1}{r} \frac{\partial(A_\theta r)}{\partial r}$$

$$B_r = -\frac{\partial A_\theta}{\partial z}$$

Also

$$J_\theta = -\sigma \frac{\partial A_\theta}{\partial t} = \sigma a \omega \sin(\omega t + \phi)$$

Now

$$rB_z = a\cos(\omega t + \phi) + \frac{r \partial a}{\partial r}\cos(\omega t + \phi) - ra\frac{\partial \phi}{\partial r}\sin(\omega t + \phi)$$

and

$$B_r = \frac{\partial a}{\partial z}\cos(\omega t + \phi) + \frac{\partial \phi}{\partial z}a\sin(\omega t + \phi)$$

but the components of the force are

$$J_\theta B_z \text{ and } -J_\theta B_r \text{ from (1)}$$

Therefore:

$$J_\theta B_z = \left(\frac{a}{r} + \frac{\partial a}{\partial z} \right)\cos(\omega t + \phi)\sigma a\omega.\sin(\omega t + \phi) - a^2\sigma\omega\frac{\partial \phi}{\partial r}\sin^2(\omega t + \phi)$$

and

$$-j_\theta b_r = \frac{\partial a}{\partial z}\sigma a\omega\cos(\omega t + \phi)(\sin \omega t + \phi) - \sigma a^2\omega \sin^2(\omega t + \phi)\frac{\partial \phi}{\partial z}$$

The $\sin 2(\omega t + \phi)$ terms have a mean value of zero, hence

$$(j \times B) = a_r J_\theta B_z = a_z J_\theta B_r$$

$$= -\tfrac{1}{2}\sigma a^2 \omega \left(1 - \cos 2(\omega t + \phi)\left[a_r\frac{\partial \phi}{\partial z} + a_z\frac{\partial \phi}{\partial r} \right] \right)$$

Hence

$$F_{\text{mean}} = (J \times B)_{\text{mean}} = -\tfrac{1}{2}\sigma a^2 \omega [\nabla \phi] \qquad (3)$$

Now by definition $S = \operatorname{curl} F$

$$\operatorname{curl} F = -\tfrac{1}{2}\sigma\omega \operatorname{curl} a^2\nabla\phi = -\tfrac{1}{2}\sigma\omega[\nabla a^2 \times \nabla\phi + a^2\nabla \times \nabla\phi]$$

$$= -\tfrac{1}{2}\sigma\omega 2a\nabla a \times \nabla\phi \quad (\text{since } \nabla \times \nabla\phi = 0)$$

Note

$$\nabla a = a_z\frac{\partial a}{\partial r} + a_z\frac{\partial a}{\partial z} \text{ and } \nabla\phi = a_r\frac{\partial\phi}{\partial r} + a_z\frac{\partial\phi}{\partial z}$$

$$\nabla a \times \nabla\phi = \begin{vmatrix} a_r & a_\theta & a_z \\ \dfrac{\partial a}{\partial r} & 0 & \dfrac{\partial a}{\partial z} \\ \dfrac{\partial\phi}{\partial r} & 0 & \dfrac{\partial\phi}{\partial z} \end{vmatrix} = a_\theta\left(\frac{\partial a}{\partial z}\frac{\partial\phi}{\partial r} - \frac{\partial a}{\partial r}\frac{\partial\phi}{\partial z}\right)$$

Hence $S = |\operatorname{curl} F| = \sigma\omega a\left(\dfrac{\partial\phi}{\partial z}\dfrac{\partial a}{\partial r} - \dfrac{\partial\phi}{\partial r}\dfrac{\partial a}{\partial z}\right).$ QED

MM5

Discuss the role of the channel furnace in an iron foundry and describe the difference between a drum furnace and a vertical channel furnace.

Describe how temperature time plots associated with a given furnace can be used to predict the output of a foundry using that furnace.

Figures MM5/1 and MM5/2 show typical holding powers required for channel furnaces and calculated superheating rates for iron.

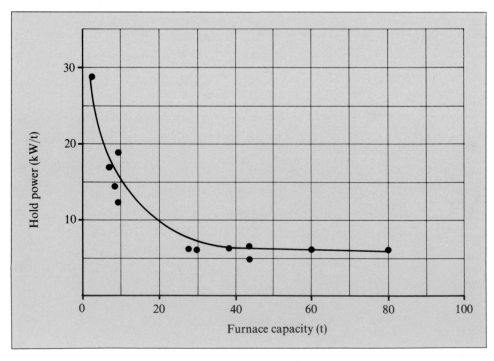

Figure MM5/1   *Holding power required for various industrial channel furnaces — melting furnaces not included.*

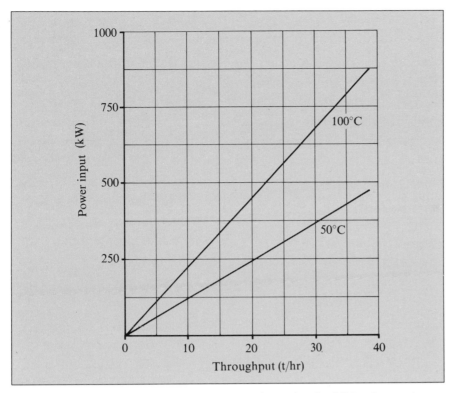

Figure MM5/2 *Calculated superheating rates obtained with additional power inputs above that to hold temperature.*

Using these graphs or otherwise determine patterns of metal temperature against time given the following circumstances:

i)   Iron is to be delivered from a channel furnace in the range 1450–1500 °C.

ii) The first configuration requires a furnace capacity of 25 t (20 t useful), the addition of 10 t metal at 1450 °C to fill the furnace (the balance being at 1500 °C), and the delivery of 10 t metal when 1500 °C is attained. You may assume there is sufficient power to heat 10 tph through 50 °C.

iii) The second configuration is similar to ii) with the difference that 2.5 t of metal is added at 1450 °C and 2.5 t of metal tapped when 1500 °C is achieved.

iv) The third configuration uses a furnace of 15 t capacity (10 t useful), 10 t of metal at 1450 °C is added to the furnace (with the balance being at 1500 °C) and the delivery of 10 t when 1500 °C is attained. Again you may assume there is sufficient power to heat 10 tph through 50 °C.

v)   The fourth configuration is similar to iv) with the difference that 2.5 t of metal is added at 1450 °C and 2.5 t of metal tapped when 1500 °C is achieved.

(The author)

129

Solution

The background to this question will be found in reference 53.

The simplest application of a channel furnace is to hold a volume of metal at a constant temperature, the energy input being chosen to equal the energy losses from the system. In this situation, it is unwise to select a furnace of excessive power rating since this will be associated with an increased conducted heat loss from an unnecessarily large metal loop and inductor box. An obvious design feature in such an application is the use of heavily insulated refractories, both in the inductor box and furnace bath, but it is now commonly accepted that relatively steep temperature gradients through the hot face material is important in reducing both refractory wear and metal penetration which, should they occur, increase the heat losses from the metal anyway. Hence, modern practice is not to maximise insulation behind the hot face refractory.

The effect of furnace capacity on the holding power required per tonne of metal stored is shown in Figure MM5/1, which has been prepared from data provided by several UK iron founders. These results, covering several furnace manufacturers, indicate fairly similar heat losses per tonne with furnace capacities exceeding 25 tonnes. Thus the inductor power may be considered only in relation to overcoming circuit inefficiencies and standing heat losses.

In order to decide on the optimum storage capacity of a channel furnace, each foundry has to assess its own requirements carefully. This decision making necessitates an accurate knowledge of the rate at which metal will be supplied to the furnace, taking account of the frequency of melting plant downtime and its duration, together with the expected demand from the moulding tracks and their possible downtime frequency and durations. Simulation of these foundry operations will then allow the optimisation of channel furnace storage capacity, noting that increased capital and running costs are associated with increased channel furnace capacity. This approach is to be recommended, being much sounder than the often used empirical solution of choosing the channel furnace to store one hour's production from the melting units.

Because of the extra heat losses incurred with worn refractory linings, badly fitting lids or incompletely dried refractories found immediately after priming with liquid metal, the values of power quoted by manufacturers to simply retain metal temperature are wisely treated as minimum values when choosing furnace rating, and should be exceeded rather than adhered to precisely. However, as already noted, there are penalties in selecting an excessive high power rating.

With a metal surface which is reasonably slag-free and contained in a well-sealed body, the power input required to hold temperature in a given channel furnace is fairly insensitive to the quantity of metal in storage. It is, therefore, sensible to retain a fairly full furnace during periods of minimum supervision, since an incorrect power input (compared to the exact value required to maintain temperature) then has minimal effect on undesirable bath heating or cooling rate. Heat losses are largely governed by body case temperature and, because the body refractories have a high inertia to temperature change, it follows that much of the energy saved by reducing power input over a weekend is largely taken from the hotter end of the refractory wall. This energy then has to be returned during the following working week and the overall energy saving is often negligible. The conclusion that the furnace is best left full of metal at its normal tapping temperature, however, may be modified in practice by metallurgical considerations.

The specific heat of liquid iron is relatively low, being around 0.22 kWh/t per °C. Once sufficient power is applied to a channel furnace to balance heat losses, further power input is converted to superheat metal at an efficiency of some 95%. This energy transfer efficiency is virtually independent of the base temperature which accounts for the economic strength of the unit in comparison with, say, a cupola for superheating iron.

Power requirements, above that to maintain metal temperature, are shown in Figure MM5/2 for two selected superheat levels and a range of metal throughout. More generally for a superheating range 8°C, specific heat C, kWh/t per °C and a metal delivery (and acceptance) rate of T t/h, the inductor rating is given by:

$$P = \frac{\theta \times C \times T + H}{\eta}$$

where H is the holding power, kW and η is the circuit efficiency.

Because the energy transferred to the inductor loop is independent of the quantity of metal contained in the furnace (assuming the minimum heel is exceeded), it follows that the temperature rise observed in the bath is dependent not only upon the power applied but also upon the quantity of metal contained in the furnace. It must be noted that the batch charging of metal to be superheated also will effect the temperature of metal tapped from the furnace and the extent of this temperature fluctuation depends upon the temperatures of the incoming metal and that already in the furnace, together with their relative quantities. The specific situations requested are plotted in Figures MM5/3 and MM5/4. The thermal inertia of the refractories has been ignored.

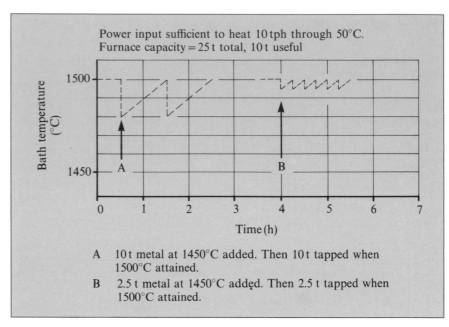

Figure MM5/3.

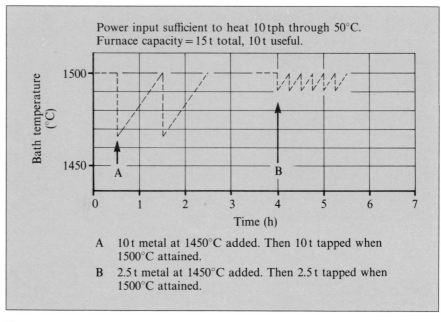

Figure MM5/4.

Clearly, the only situation which provides a constant metal temperature at the spout of the furnace is that which involves a continuous and steady stream of metal (at a uniform temperature) being fed at the same rate as a continuous metal off-take, provided that the energy required for superheating is precisely applied. As soon as these criteria are not adhered to, then metal bath temperature fluctuations occur. With the batch charging of liquid metal to be superheated, fall in bath temperature is inevitable and, for a given superheat requirement, the temperature fall which is acceptable can only be obtained by the correct selection of the weight of metal added relative to the quantity of metal already contained within the furnace. These effects are demonstrated in Figures MM5/3 and MM5/4 which show the results of two charged metal weights (10 t and 2.5 t) added to two levels of residual metal in the furnace (15 t and 5 t).

From the above it can be seen that temperature time plots can produce a pictorial assessment of the output of the furnaces chosen given known circumstances of charging and dispensing liquid metal. Such plots can be extended to include other factors such as the influence of delays due to breakdowns.

Plots such as these combined with power-time plots and metal availability-time plots can be used in computer simulations which are now part of the required mechanism in designing a new foundry.

MM6

Describe some of the advantages of using solid state frequency converters in the range 500 Hz–10 kHz to feed coreless furnaces. Table 1 compares a medium frequency with a mains frequency furnace.

Table 1

	Medium frequency	Mains frequency
Furnace capacity	4 tonnes	12 tonnes
Installed power	3000 kW	3000 kW
Frequency	500 Hz	50 Hz
Standing heat losses (lid on) averaged over complete melt cycle	47 kW	160 kW
Power supply efficiency (to the furnace coil)	96%	97%
Coil efficiency	80%	80%
Bath diameter	930 mm	1140 mm

Table 2 compares the operating cycle possible from each.

Table 2

	Medium frequency (minutes)	Mains frequency (minutes)
1. Melting power-on time	40	39
2. Time lost for charging	4	4
3. Deslagging, temperature and analysis measurement time	5	5.5
4. Tapping time	2	2.5
5. Total cycle time	51 mins	51 min

Discuss some of the advantages and disadvantages of each type of furnace.

(*The author*)

Solution

Background to the first part is given in reference 54.

The student might be expected to list some of the following factors:

a)   Frequency conversion by solid state involves lower capital cost than rotary alternatives, at least at the frequencies required by the foundry industry.

b)   The solid state power device, because of its ability to provide a swinging frequency, provides a more constant level of energy input to the workpiece as its inductive reactance changes, without having to install the switchable capacitors required with a rotary set.

c) The solid state device is comparatively light in weight and is vibration free.

d) The inverter has no moving parts and requires no maintenance. Not containing any large components, it is also comparatively easy to replace defective items.

e) Stopping and starting of the solid state converter does not involve much extra stress on the components and standby losses can therefore be virtually eliminated.

f) The efficiency of energy conversion in the frequency converter can exceed 95% in the solid state system but is less than 90% for a rotary set. This efficiency remains good even at low output power levels from the solid state device.

g) Single phase to three phase conversion is inherent in the solid state converter (compared with mains frequency systems).

h) Medium frequencies offer higher power densities with lower thermal losses.

i) Stirring is less violent in medium frequency furnaces than in mains frequency furnaces.

A comparison of the two tables should lead to the following conclusions and expectations:

1) The medium frequency furnace is smaller volumetrically than its mains frequency counterpart. From this it may be deduced:

  i) Civil engineering costs of installing would be lower.

  ii) Thermal losses will be lower and hence the total kWh required for melting will be lower for the medium frequency unit.

  iii) Although the cycle time is the same the mains frequency unit will require special start-up and run-down arrangements. The medium frequency can melt from a cold scrap charge and therefore is able to operate within a single shift. The larger mains frequency unit is better geared towards 3 shift working.

2) If the foundry metal demand can be so arranged to minimise waiting or holding times then the medium frequency system will be preferred.

3) Variability of iron specification is best met by the smaller medium frequency unit.

4) Operational cycles can be more readily changed using medium frequency units than with mains frequency units. For example, Figure MM6/1 shows that comparable kWh consumptions can only be achieved using three shift operation with the mains frequency unit.

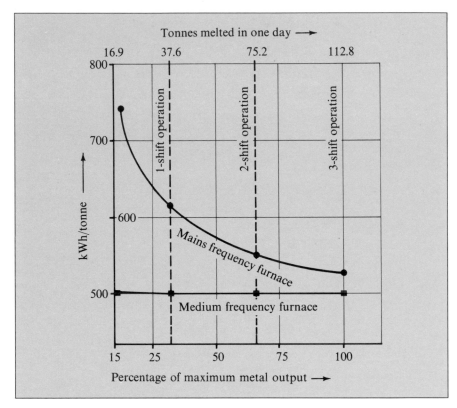

Figure MM6/1 *Calculated energy required to produce various daily throughputs of molten iron from a medium frequency and a mains frequency coreless furnace.*

MM7

What is the likely relationship between the metal velocity of the melt in a coreless furnace and the electromagnetic force field set up in the melt by the working coil current. Determine a suitable expression relating metal velocity with field in the meniscus.

Prove that if P is the absorbed power into the melt, H is the field and f the applied frequency

$$P \propto f^{1/2}.H^2$$

From these expressions (or otherwise) link the metal stirring force to applied frequency and power.

(The author)

Solution
Metal velocity is associated with electromagnetic force by a rough proportionality.

(i) *Simple proof*

Consider a coreless furnace with its bath and coil. The stirring patterns will be shown in the form of a vortex. It will be assumed that the melt is fluid and that the effects of viscosity variation may be ignored.

A particle within the melt at the neutral point of the vortex where the $J \times B$ force is a maximum will have a velocity V.

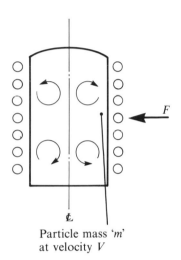

Particle mass 'm'
at velocity V

The force to stop it will be

$$F = k.\frac{m}{r}.V^2$$

where m is the particle mass

          r is its effective centripetal radius

          k is a constant

The force F is electromagnetic such that

$F = k' \times$ coil current $\times$ work piece current

$\quad = K' \times I^2$

$\quad = K \times H^2$

where k, K', K are constants

      I is coil current.

From which we obtain

$$F = k.\frac{m}{r}.V^2 = K \times H^2$$

or approximately

metal velocity is proportional to field strength   QED

(ii) *More direct proof* (modified by the author from reference 55)

The time smoothed Navier-Stokes equation may be written

$$c[u.\nabla]u = -\nabla p + \nabla.\bar{\tau} + [\overline{J \times B}] \tag{1}$$

where ∇p is the pressure gradient

    u is metal velocity

    $\bar{\tau}$ is the stress tensor

    C is specific density of metal

Because we are concerned with circulatory flows due to the rotational part of the electromagnetic force field then taking the curl of equation (1):

$$c\nabla \times [u.\nabla]u = \nabla \times \nabla.\bar{\tau} + \nabla \times [\overline{J \times B}] \tag{2}$$

It can be shown that the term involving the shear stress is an order of magnitude smaller than the inertial and electromagnetic force terms in a region near the refractory wall.

Thus

$$c\nabla \times [u.\nabla]u \doteqdot \nabla \times [\overline{J \times B}] \tag{3}$$

If B_0 is the maximum value of the field near the wall along the length over which the field and metal velocity change, then

$$c\nabla \times [u.\nabla]u \doteqdot c\bar{U}_0{}^2 \tag{4}$$

and

$$\nabla \times (\overline{J \times B}) \doteqdot \frac{B_0{}^2}{\mu} \tag{5}$$

μ is permeability and U_0 is maximum velocity.

Hence

$$\bar{U}_0{}^2 \doteqdot \frac{B_0{}^2}{\mu c} \tag{6}$$

and

$$\bar{U}_0 = k.B_0 \tag{7}$$

QED

Proof of $P\alpha f^{1/2}.H^2$

Consider the melt to be cylindrical of diameter D and length L.

The depth of penetration is given by

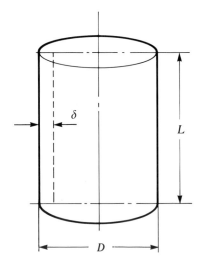

$$\delta = \sqrt{\frac{2\rho}{\mu_0.\mu_r.2\pi f}} \tag{8}$$

ρ is resistivity.

Now

$$P = I^2.R \tag{9}$$

where R is resistance of effective current path.

$$R = \frac{\rho.\pi.D}{\delta L} \tag{10}$$

From which combining 8, 9 and 10 we obtain

$$P\alpha f^{1/2}.H^2 \tag{11}$$

(the constant of proportionality is a function of furnace size).

Now stirring force is the measure of metal movement.

138

Hence combining equations 7 and 11

$$\text{`Stirring'} \; \alpha \frac{P^{1/2}}{f^{1/4}}$$

In practice

$$\text{`Stirring'} \; \alpha \frac{P^{1/2}}{f^{n}}$$

and n is between 1/4 and 1.

MM8

Using the findings of example MM7 deduce an expression for current density in the melt of a coreless furnace as a function of meniscus height.

For a given melt and temperature show that the electrical 'losses' in the melt remain constant with constant meniscus height.

(*The author*)

Solution

Stirring force $\alpha \dfrac{P^{1/2}}{f^{1/4}}$ (using symbols defined earlier).

$$\text{Volume of melt} \doteqdot \frac{\pi d^2}{4}.h.$$

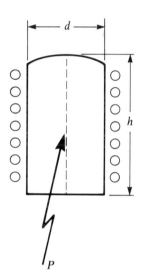

Maximum cross section in the vertical plane

$= \pi d.h$ and the power density $P' = \dfrac{P}{\pi.d.h}$

$$d = 2 \times \sqrt{\frac{V}{\pi h}} \qquad \therefore \quad P' = \frac{K}{\sqrt{h}}$$

Taking $\dfrac{d}{\delta} > 8$ and because $P' = \dfrac{\rho.H^2}{\delta}.p$

$$p = \frac{2}{\left[1.23 + \dfrac{d}{\delta}\right]}$$

$$\therefore \quad P' = \frac{\rho.H^2}{\delta.4}\left[= \frac{K}{\sqrt{h}}\right]$$

or

$$H^2 = \frac{c'}{\sqrt{h}}$$

Now

$$H = \frac{I}{h} \quad \text{(ampere turns/metre)}$$

and

$$\frac{I^2}{h^2} = \frac{c'}{\sqrt{h}} \quad \ldots\ldots \; c' \text{ is a constant.}$$

$$\therefore \quad I = c'h^{3/4} \quad \text{but} \quad J = \frac{I}{\delta \times h}$$

from which

$$\delta h J = c'h^{3/4}$$

or

$$J = \frac{k}{h^{1/4}}$$

Now the 'losses' in the melt

$$= \pi.d.h. \quad \delta \quad .\rho.I^2$$
$$\text{(area) (depth)}$$

$$= \pi.d.h.\delta.\rho.J^2.\delta^2 h^2$$

$$= \pi.d.h^3.\delta^3.\rho.J^2$$

$$= \pi.d.h^3.\delta^3.\rho.\frac{k^2}{h^{1/2}}$$

$$\doteqdot K''.h^{5/2}$$

where K'', K''' are constants

$$\doteqdot K'''''$$

if h is 'constant'.   QED

CHAPTER 7

Arc furnaces for steel melting

7.1 Background to the teaching

It is an interesting speculation to make that as a developed country reaches what is now termed the post-industrialisation phase so the internal demand for steel reduces. If the situation is reached where scrap availability equals or exceeds steel demand then the tonnage requirements should conveniently be met by scrap melting. No contemporary mechanism for tonnage scrap melting readily competes with the direct arc furnace and although over the years fuel-oxygen convertors have been proposed the arc furnace remains internationally the pre-eminent scrap melter.

In this case no apology is made for the fact that in the UK tonnage arc furnaces will remain few in number [<100]. However in common with other melting furnaces there is wonderful scope for using the furnace as an example of interdisciplinary involvement. The furnace can be used to explore voltage current locii, to introduce the concept of non-linear impedance, as a source of system disturbances, as a convenient exercise in energy-use strategy and returning to its *real* use an example of metallurgical processing involving material and thermal/energy balances combined with production scheduling.

Again Robiette[51] provides a convenient first source. In the mid-seventies a conference was convened to review the status of the furnace[56] at which the author presented a detailed approach to the status of the process. This work emphasised the need for an up to date teaching document and the monograph by Swinden[57] meets this requirement.

Power supply engineers do tend to become excited with arc furnaces — where else can 80 MW become 80 MVAr (or nothing) in less than half a cycle? — and their concern with the flicker phenomenon and its measurement has probably given rise to more papers than for other arc-furnace issues. The author's own review of the subject[58] is still relevant the only measurable progress made since those days lying in the use of complex flicker meters each with their own adherents. In terms of teaching the fundamentals the ERA work of the sixties[59] can be helpful at the second year undergraduate stage. The position in the UK is now defined within an appropriate engineering recommendation[60].

As an interesting example of control engineering there are few equals and examples are given which emphasise this interest.

As with the previous chapter examples are given which follow a tutorial assignment pattern.

7.2 List of worked examples

AF1

Describe how you would conduct a short circuit test on an arc furnace explaining what particular furnace conditions must prevail and what precautions you would take.

A 25 t 25 MVA (nominal) steel making arc furnace is subjected to short circuit tests. On the top secondary tap of 300 volts/line to neutral (or furnace bath) the average phase voltage on short circuit is 275 volts and the average electrode current is 40 kA. The average phase angle is measured as 82.8° at short circuit. Using these data construct a circle diagram and from it determine the maximum power input possible and the current at which this occurs. If the current corresponding to the transformer continuous rating is 21 kA what instructions would you expect to issue to the electricians setting the breaker?

You may neglect transformer losses.

(The author)

Solution
Furnace condition is flat bath of molten metal.

Select appropriate tap on furnace secondary. Use 3 wattmeter method on secondary using furnace CT's and line to neutral. *KEEP NEUTRAL FLOATING.* Take care with CT and PT ratios.

Lower one electrode into bath on manual, lower second electrode into bath then lower third into bath again on manual. Switch to automatic and let electrode controller clear. As third electrode makes contact read wattmeters. In practice best to photograph wattmeters!

Repeat for each voltage tap.

The method which follows is described by Robiette[51] and is discussed by Ravenscroft[61].

The arc furnace circuit may be represented as a simple series circuit consisting of inductance and resistance, representing the transformer flexibles and busbars and a variable resistance representing the arc. Such a circuit fed from a constant input voltage has a current locus of a semi-circle.

The locus may be determined for a given transformer voltage tap by determining experimentally the short circuit current I_2 and its associated phase angle

$$\phi_s = \left[\cos^{-1} \frac{MW_{sc}}{MVA_{sc}} \right] \qquad \text{see Figure AF1}$$

144

The line $I_s X$ tangential to OI_s defines Ox as the diameter of the required semi-circle locus. All operating powers of the furnace lie on arc OI_s and from this locus circuit power, overall electrical efficiency, circuit power factor and arc power can be deduced.

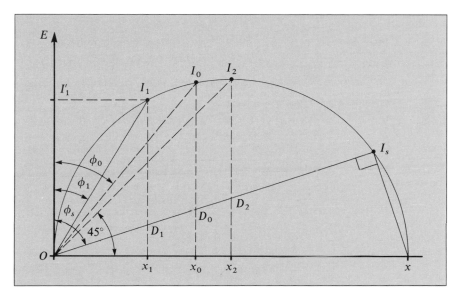

Figure AF1 *The current-locus diagram for an arc furnace*

Consider an operating condition I_1 then power factor is $\cos \phi_1$, the current OI_1 and the power $\sqrt{3}.OE.OI_1{}'$. Thus a graph of power against current can be drawn. Again the quantity $\sqrt{3}.OE.D_1 I_1$ represents the power dissipated by the arc. The maximum input power is determined by making $xOI_2 = 45°$ and calculating $\sqrt{3}.OE.I_2 x_2$. Note that $\sqrt{3}.OE.D_2 I_2$ is not the maximum arc power — this quantity is determined by making $\phi_0 = \phi_s/2$ and calculating $\sqrt{3}.OE.I_0 D_0$ (the suffix o denoting 'optimum'). It will be appreciated that this construction gives the maximum abscissa $I_0 D_0$ which of course corresponds to the maximum arc power. A further power characteristic can be drawn using the intercepts $I_n D_n$ of arc power against current. The electrical efficiency is given by $I_n D_n / I_n x_n$. The term 'optimum current' refers to that current giving maximum arc power.

Short circuit MVA $= \sqrt{3} \times 275 \times 40{,}000 \times 10^{-6}$

$$= 19\,\text{MVA}$$

Short circuit power $= 19 \times \cos 82.8°$

$$= 2.38\,\text{MW}$$

Construct circle diagram using 275 volts, 40 kA and 82.8° as the base vector using an appropriate scale.

Maximum input power occurs at about 28 kA and is about 10.2 MW.

Since 28 kA exceeds the transformer continuous rating of 21 kA then the circuit breaker must be set to trip if a short circuit is maintained.

AF2

Describe the difference between direct and indirect arc furnaces. What do you understand by submerged arc furnaces and how is the heat generation and transmission different from direct arc furnaces?

A 20 t 10 MVA (nominal) fed at 33 kV steelmaking arc furnace is subjected to a short circuit test by electrode dipping. The results show that at short circuit 17.05 MVA, and 2.755 MW are drawn from the system with an average current of 37.9 kA/electrode. Construct a circle diagram and from it determine the maximum power that can be delivered by the arcs and the phase current in the arcs when the furnace is drawing the maximum power. Ignore system regulation.

(*The author*)

Solution

Direct arc is from electrode(s) to bath.

Indirect is from electrode to electrode over bath.

Submerged arc furnaces have electrodes dipped in ore gangue continually so heat generation is resistive ($i^2 R$) and transmission is by conduction. Direct arc furnaces produce arcs so heat generation is resistive within the arc and transmitted by radiation.

The problem is merely a variation on the use of the current locus given in the earlier example AF1.

In this case the voltage-current locus is drawn so that

$$\phi_{sc} = \cos^{-1} \left| \frac{2.755}{17.05} \right| = 80.70°$$

$$I_{sc} = \frac{17.05 \times 10^6}{\sqrt{3 \times 33 \times 10^3}} = 298 \text{ A}$$

This value corresponds to the given 37.9 kA per electrode. 33 kV is used because the voltage drop can be ignored.

Then the construction gives 8.7 MW, 7.14 MW and an arc current for maximum arc power of about 27.1 kA.

AF3

i) Draw an equivalent single-phase circuit for an arc furnace when connected to the electricity supply system. Relate the equivalent circuit components to physical system components and describe what approximations, if any, are made.

ii) A short-circuit test is carried out on a 3-phase arc furnace. The point-of-common-coupling (PCC) voltage is 50 kV/line to line and the short-circuit phase current is 363 A. The power input is 3.56 MW. What are the total power losses at maximum input power and maximum output power?

At maximum output power, what is the equivalent resistance/ph of the arc?

iii) If system regulation is taken into consideration (assume inductive reactance), 'recalculate' the power losses at maximum input and output power. (NB: source voltage = 52 kV/line to line, power input at supply is 4 MW for the short circuit situation.)

(Courtesy of the University of Aston)

Solution

Part (i)

An equivalent single phase diagram provides a convenient approach to assessing the capability of the supply network to feed the arc furnace. The arc furnace will normally have its supply transformer, secondary bus-bars to the electrodes along an axis normal to the slagging and tapping lines. The three electrodes will normally be on an equilateral triangle with the 'centre' electrode either away from the transformer or near it. Either configuration will produce phase to phase asymmetry which in practice can be as much as 30% of the mean phase secondary impedance. An equivalent single-phase diagram will thus ignore this asymmetry and the phase-phase interdependence. It is normal to refer all the constituent components of the circuit to the supply system or arc furnace transformer primary and to identify their position to the point of common coupling (P_{cc}) with other loads.

In this case the equivalent circuit may be drawn as shown.

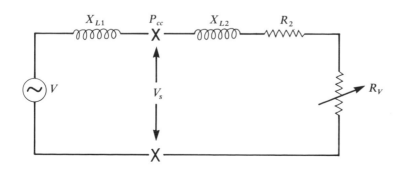

All quantities referred to PRIMARY.

V The nominal voltage at a point of generation per phase.

V_s The nominal supply voltage at the point of common coupling per phase.

V_{s1} The nominal supply voltage at the point of common coupling line to line.

X_{L1} The source impedance, usually assumed to be inductive, to include generation, transmission lines, transformers and other passive elements between the point of generation and the point of common coupling.

X_{L2} The load reactance representing elements comprising the furnace and its transformers. Phase to phase mutual dependence and asymmetry make this an approximation.

R_2 The load resistance associated with X_{L2} and excluding the arc impedance — again an approximation.

R_V A variable resistance representing the arc. Arc impedance is difficult to represent and this approximation permits a number of fixed points to be examined (eg $R_V = 0$ corresponds to shorting electrodes to the bath and $R_V = \infty$ corresponds to open circuit conditions). Again if R_V is allowed to vary perhaps sinusoidally this represents a 'flicker' effect.

Part (ii)

$$V_{s1} = 50\,\text{kV line to line}$$

Short circuit current $I_{sc} = 363\,\text{A per phase}$

The total power $P = 3.56\,\text{MW}$

$$P = \sqrt{3}.V_{s1}.I \cos \phi$$

and
$$\cos \phi_{sc} = \frac{3.56 \times 10^6}{\sqrt{3} \times 50 \times 10^3 \times 363}$$

$$= 0.113 \text{ giving } \phi_{sc} = 83.5°$$

A plot of MW against MVAr can be drawn (Figure AF3/1) and the short circuit vector OZ_{sc} constructed. The points of maximum input power and maximum output can be taken from the circle diagram, as described in example AF1.

Maximum input power occurs with $\phi_2 = 45°$

Giving losses $= 1.9\,\text{MW}$ (from locus)

Maximum output power occurs with $\phi_s = \dfrac{\phi_{sc}}{2} = 41.75°$

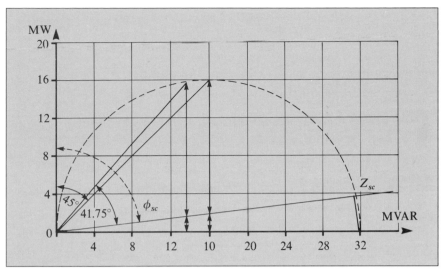

Figure AF 3/1

Giving losses = 1.6 MW (from locus)

Maximum arc power = 14 MW (from locus)

Power per phase $= \dfrac{14}{3} = 4.67$ MW

Total MVA = 20.6 (from locus) at the maximum arc power
condition. Thus the arc resistance is given by

$$R = \dfrac{4.67 \times 10^6}{\left[\dfrac{20.6 \times 10^6}{50 \times 10^3 \times \sqrt{3}}\right]^2}$$

$$= 82.5 \text{ ohms per phase}$$

Part (iii)
In the case where system regulation is considered a new circle
diagram is plotted (figure AF3/2)

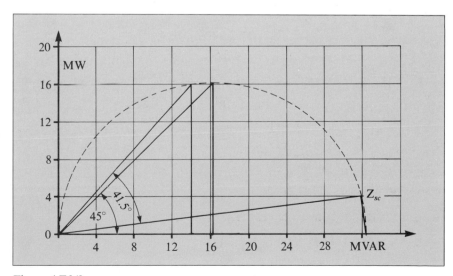

Figure AF 3/2

$$\cos \phi_{sc} = \frac{4 \times 10^6}{\sqrt{3} \times 52 \times 10^3 \times 363}$$

and $\qquad\qquad \phi_{sc} = 83°$

(it is, of course, assumed that the short circuit current remains the same).

Again, the vector OZ_{sc} can be plotted giving the power losses for maximum input power as 2.0 MW and at maximum output power as 1.8 MW from the graph.

AF4

Describe the term short-circuit voltage depression in relationship to a power system feeding an arc furnace. What do you understand by gauge point fluctuation voltage and severity factor?

Find the percentage voltage depression for a 10 MVA furnace fed from a fault level of 1000 MVA. Explain the MVA swing chosen. If the severity factor is 0.12 calculate gauge point fluctuation voltage.

(*The author*)

Solution

A detailed treatment is given in references 59 and 60.

Short circuit voltage depression V_t is defined from the equation:

$$V_t = \left(\frac{S_t}{S_c}\right) \times 100\%$$

where S_t is the short circuit arc furnace MVA
$\qquad$ S_c is the network short circuit power at point of common coupling.

Gauge point fluctuation voltage is that flicker voltage exceeding 1% of the time expressed as a percentage of rms supply voltage.

Severity factor is an empirical term linking the 1% gauge point to V_t. Thus $V_{fg} = K_s . V_t$ where V_{fg} is 1% gauge point voltage and K_s is severity factor.

Most furnaces have a SCMVA $= 2/2.5$ times nominal MVA.

$$\therefore \quad \text{in example } V_t = \left(\frac{2.5 \times 10}{1000}\right) \times 100 = 2.5\%$$

$$V_{fg} = 0.12 \times 2.5 = 0.3\%$$

AF5

Describe a typical arc furnace electrode control system. What is meant by an arc impedance control?

In an attempt to obtain true arc impedance control consideration is to be given to determining arc voltage by assessing the circuit voltage drops to the electrode tips. What are the pitfalls — give a simple analysis?

What problems arise in trying to superimpose a control criterion of constant phase power and constant energy consumed per electrode? What is the inherent reason?

(The author)

Solution

The first part of the question will emerge from the quoted references. The definition of arc impedance control and the argument underlying the two issues discussed in the rest of the question arises from the following reasoning:

Once the transformer tap has been selected the only control of the arc circuit that can be exerted is through electrode position control. There are many ways of achieving control all dependent on a variant of the equation:

$$\varepsilon = k_1 V_{arc} - k_2 I_{arc}$$

where ε is error, V_{arc} is arc voltage, I_{arc} is arc current, k_1, k_2 are constants.

Clearly ignoring voltage regulation effects in the arc circuits (ie putting $k_1 V_{arc} =$ constant) current control is possible and this formed the basis of the early systems. Due to the need to meet 'undervoltage' conditions the system known as arc impedance control was developed. By controlling ε to an attempted zero (a first order controller) then $V_{arc}/I_{arc} =$ constant and this is the most popular system.

There are two fundamental aspects which need examination. The arc itself is remote from easy measurement (being at the end of the electrode). It is tempting to derive I_{arc} and V_{arc} by some form of indirect measurement. Again the transformer, busbar, flexible secondary circuit will itself lead to asymmetry and if power control is attempted by, for example, a control equation of the form

$$\varepsilon = P_{ref} - k.V_{arc}.I_{arc}$$

then phase interaction will occur — the following analyses demonstrate the difficulties:

Analysis of arc voltage compensation circuits
Assuming an impedance controller working at set points V_0, I_0. Then at steady state

$$K_1 V_0 - K_2 I_0 = 0 \qquad (1)$$

At any other condition

$$K_1 V - K_2 I = \varepsilon \tag{2}$$

with ε as the control error.

One control option is to suggest that under short circuit conditions the control error signal should be such as to permit maximum electrode lift-off speed. If the set current I_0 is a fraction $1/K_3$ of the short circuited current then the maximum current is $K_3 I_0$. Let the measured short circuit voltage at that point be $K_4 V_0$, then

$$\varepsilon_{max} = K_1 K_4 V_0 - K_2 K_3 I_0 \tag{3}$$

but under these conditions if V is compensated appropriately $K_4 = 0$ (the arc is extinguished), thus

$$\varepsilon_{max}' = -K_2 K_3 I_0 \tag{4}$$

and ε_{max}' represents the maximum error if the voltage measurements were compensated correctly.

Thus the ratio of the sensitivities at short circuit:

$$\frac{\varepsilon_{max}}{\varepsilon_{max}'} = \frac{K_1 K_4 V_0 - K_2 K_3 I_0}{-K_2 K_3 I}$$

$$= 1 - \frac{K_1 K_4 V_0}{K_2 K_3 I_0}$$

$$= 1 - \frac{K_4}{K_3} \tag{5}$$

since $\dfrac{K_1 V_0}{K_2 I_0} = 1$.

From (5) it is seen that for a given gain K_4 the reduction of sensitivity is high when operating points are a significant fraction of the short circuit current. A method which has been used to nominally improve the position at short circuit is to arrange that a compensating voltage signal $K_5 I'$ is provided to give zero voltage signal, where I' may be expected to be the current at short circuit.

Then $K_1 K_4 V_0 - K_5 K_3 I_0 = 0$; $K_5 K_3 I_0$ being the compensating signal at short circuit. From which $K_5 = \dfrac{K_2 K_4}{K_3}$.

Then the error equation becomes

$$\varepsilon = [K_1 V - K_5 I] - K_2 I$$

$$= \left[K.V - \frac{K_2 K_4 I}{K_3} \right] - K_2 I \tag{6}$$

but clearly this would not give $\varepsilon = 0$ at the desired operating point $V_0 I_0$. Hence the compensated voltage signal must be increased by a further gain factor K_6 such that

$$K_6 \left[K_1 V_0 - \frac{K_2 K_4 I_0}{K_3} \right] = K_1 V_0$$

which still gives zero voltage at short circuit. From which

$$K_6 = \frac{K_3}{K_3 - K_4} \qquad (7)$$

The error equation now becomes

$$\varepsilon = \frac{K_3}{K_3 - K_4} \cdot \left[K_1 V - \frac{K_2 K_4}{K_3} I \right] - K_2 I$$

$$= \left[\frac{K_3}{(K_3 - K_4)} \right] \cdot K_1 V - \left[\frac{K_3}{(K_3 - K_4)} \right] K_2 I \qquad (8)$$

This equation merely shows that the voltage compensation is equivalent to an increase of signal level in both voltage and current channels by the factor $\dfrac{K_3}{K_3 - K_4}$ thus dispensing with complicated compensation networks.

The effects of phase impedance asymmetry on phase power[19]
Introduction
Figure AF4/1 shows a representation of a three phase load Z_1, Z_2, Z_3 fed by a star connected transformer with phase potentials e_1, e_2, e_3. Since the star point of the potential source is floating the equivalent potentials E_{12}, E_{23}, E_{31} for a delta connected transformer are obtained by simple vectorial addition.

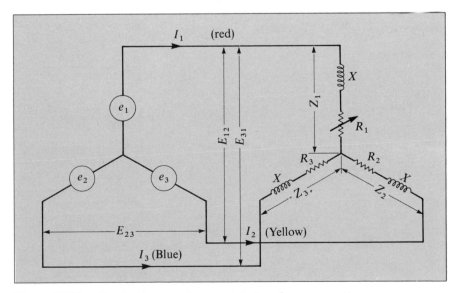

Figure AF4/1 *Circuit diagram of asymmetric impedance connections*

Method of calculation

The line currents I_R, I_B and I_Y may be shown to be:

$$I_R = \frac{E_{12}Z_3 - E_{31}Z_2}{Z_1Z_2 + Z_2Z_3 + Z_3Z_1} \tag{9}$$

$$I_Y = \frac{E_{23}Z_1 - E_{12}Z_3}{Z_1Z_2 + Z_2Z_3 + Z_3Z_1} \tag{10}$$

$$I_B = \frac{E_{31}Z_2 - E_{23}Z_1}{Z_1Z_2 + Z_2Z_3 + Z_3Z_1} \tag{11}$$

NB   It is assumed that the phase and line emfs are symmetrical and displaced by 120°.

From Figure AF4/1 the following expressions for phase powers arise:

$$P_R = E^2 R_1 \cdot \left(\frac{(R_3 + 0.5R_2 + 0.866\,X)^2 + (1.5X - 0.866R_2)^2}{(R_1R_2 + R_2R_3 + R_3R_1 - 3X^2)^2 + 4X^2(R_1 + R_2 + R_3)^2} \right) \tag{12}$$

$$P_Y = E^2 R_2 \cdot \left(\frac{(-0.5R_1 - R_3 + 0.866X)^2 + (0.866R_1 + 1.5X)^2}{(R_1R_2 + R_2R_3 + R_3R_1 - 3X^2)^2 + 4X^2(R_1 + R_2 + R_3)^2} \right) \tag{13}$$

$$P_B = E^2 R_3 \cdot \left(\frac{(0.5R_1 - 0.5R_2 - 1.732X)^2 + (0.866R_1 + 0.866R_2)^2}{(R_1R_2 + R_2R_3 + R_3R_1 - 3X^2)^2 + 4X^2(R_1 + R_2 + R_3)^2} \right) \tag{14}$$

where E is the amplitude of line voltage (rms).

Equations (12), (13) and (14) allow for variations in R_1, R_2 and R_3 but the inductance per phase (X) is assumed to be equal and constant.

The relation between P_R, P_Y and P_B will obviously be affected by the power factor of the circuit in each phase. The following calculation determining dimensionless power is based on an initially balanced three phase impedance with a power factor of 0.8. The effect of varying the red phase resistance is considered, the resistances of the other two phases remaining equal and at a value of unity. Thus:

R_1 is a variable quantity on a per unit basis,

$R_2 = R_3 =$ the unit value of R_1,

$jX = j0.75$ of the unit value of R_1,

E is assumed to be unity (on a per unit basis).

Equations (12), (13) and (14) may now be simplified:

$$P_R = \frac{4.7R_1}{6.25R_1{}^2 + 6.25R_1 + 9.47} \tag{15}$$

$$P_Y = \frac{R_1{}^2 + 2.3R_1 + 1.38}{6.25R_1{}^2 + 6.25R_1 + 9.47} \tag{16}$$

$$P_B = \frac{R_1{}^2 - 0.3R_1 + 4}{6.25R_1{}^2 + 6.25R_1 + 9.47} \tag{17}$$

Discussion of results

Figure AF4/2 shows a plot of the phase powers P_R, P_Y and P_B for variations in R_1 between 0.1 and 50 ($R_2 = R_3$ remaining fixed at the unity value of R_1).

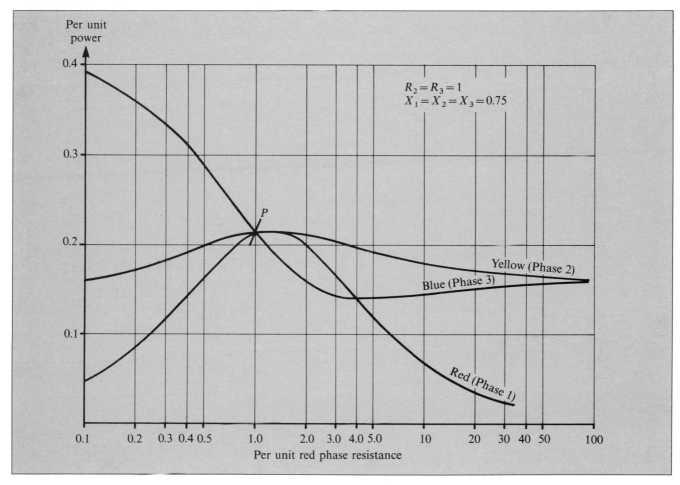

Figure AF4/2 *Theoretical curves showing distribution of phase powers for variations in red phase resistance*

Even though an arc furnace equivalent circuit cannot be represented in terms of linear resistances, it is considered that the results demonstrate the interdependence between phase powers. The non-linearity of the furnace arc will cause a difference between theoretical and practical results. Whereas in the theoretical case the phase impedance in the yellow and blue phases is assumed to remain constant the corresponding furnace impedances will be modified to an extent dependent on the change in current in those phases. Even though the electrode regulators will try to compensate for this and maintain a constant phase impedance the resulting ratio X/R in those phases will be altered. Thus, the practical case defies quantitative analysis in the absence of accurate data on the fundamental behaviour of a furnace arc. It has been found that there is close agreement between this theory and the trends in actual practice.

The curves shown in Figure AF4/2 are plotted for a positive phase sequence. At P change in arc resistance in the red phase has little effect on the power in either the red (1) or yellow (2) phases. The blue phase (3) power is significantly affected and the possibility arises that control may be achieved by varying the red phase resistance to control blue phase power, yellow phase resistance to control red phase power and so on. This is the philosophy by which electrode position control can be adapted to give power control.

AF6

Two large electric arc steelmaking furnaces each rated at 15 MW are to operate a production schedule within a maximum demand level of 20 MW measured over a period of 30 minutes. Discuss the impact of such a restriction on metal production.

This industrial load has a measured maximum demand limit of 20 MW. The controlled period is 30 minutes. In a given half an hour period the load taken is:

Time	8	10	12	14	16	18	22	16 minutes
MW	6	6.5	7	7.5	7.9	8.0	8.8	8.4

If you were a fuel controller what action would you have advised at the 12th and 18th minutes to maximise the use of electricity?

(The author)

Solution
This example may be extended to cover any group of sheddable loads. In this form two furnaces are working more or less independently. Clearly, however, the cost per kVA of maximum demand for the unrestricted situation (30 MW) may not be justified during peak periods of tariff costs. Here the steelmaker has selected (inferentially) a maximum demand level of 20 MW.

Sometimes maximum demand is quoted in MW sometimes in MVA (it is now more normal in MVA) at a quoted price of £x per kW (or kVA). Power (or kVA) in this context is defined as being the number of units (kWh) used in a measured half hour period multiplied by $2^{9.13}$. Thus in this example a target maximum demand of 20 MW corresponds to the use of 10,000 kWh (10 MWh) in a measured half hour period.

Having decided this MD target the tactics of controlling the load within the target may be defined. Initially in any period there need

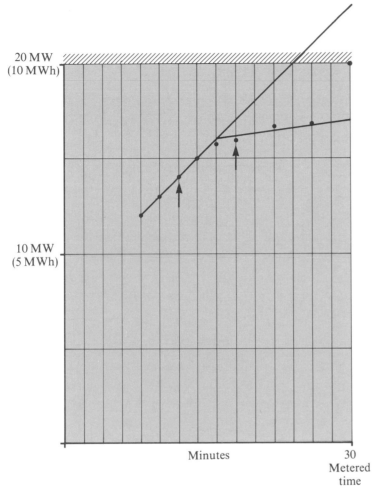

NOTE: The MWh reading would not be 'printed' until end
       of $\frac{1}{2}$ hour, e.g. at minute $12 = 14$ MW at that
       metered time if load drops to zero. $\therefore$ Multiply
       each given reading by two.

Answers
 (i) Load shed 5 MW (actual load 15 MW, ideal
     load $= 10$ MW)
(ii) Increase 7.0 MW (actual load 3 MW, ideal
     load $= 10$ MW)

Important
 (i) Ignore readings after 12th min.
(ii) Ignore readings after 18th min.

be no constraints on the loads but as the period progresses an
assessment can be made as to whether the target will be under or
overshot. This assessment made continuously either manually (but
more likely automatically) can determine whether load should be
shed or increased (if desired). The financial penalty for exceeding
the agreed target could be severe.

A further complication (not relevant to this example) is that for
non-peak periods there may (or may not) be a different and lower
cost of maximum demand, or none at all, and the price per unit
(kWh) will also be lower.

This example ignores the detailed financial situation and asks the student to work to a stated MD level.

Clearly two furnaces operating completely independently would require (in the limit) a maximum demand of 30 MW. However the peak power demand is usually required only during the melting periods. For a typical melting cycle the ratio

$$\frac{\text{time for maximum demand}}{\text{total tap to tap time}}$$

for such furnaces seldom exceeds, individually 50%, the balance of the time being at either zero power during, for example, charging and tapping times and short maintenance breaks or at a level perhaps no more than 25% of the maximum power during refining. Clearly the imposition of a 20 MW limit will reduce the maximum metal production but properly scheduled the reduction is not likely to exceed 10%.

By plotting dynamically a plot of kWh accepted over the metered MD period (30 minutes) and measuring appropriate slopes relevant *power* data can be obtained. For example, the slope of the line connecting the instantaneous point with the target point will produce an estimate of the load which can be accepted to meet the MD target.

The example uses just such a plot to obtain the stated actions at the prescribed times.

Lasers

CHAPTER 8

8.1 Background to the teaching

In this present context lasers are treated as a particular example of a high intensity power source. The teaching monograph by Milne (62) provides a brief but relevant introduction to the subject. Other introductions by Harry (lesson 11, reference 6 and reference 63) are helpful. For those wishing more detailed treatments, Svelto (64) provides a reasonable compromise between a practical and theoretical treatment and the work by Siegman (65) has some relevant material.

Perhaps a fundamental requirement is to be able to determine the properties of beam focusing and the power densities achievable and this involves the fundamentals of optics (66, 67).

8.2 The worked examples

L1

Describe the process of pumping as applied to lasers. Differentiate between optical and electrical pumping. Why is optical pumping not usually suitable for gas lasers?

The radiative output from a 10 kW CO_2 laser occurs at a wavelength (λ) of 10.6 μm. The beam is focused using a lens of focal length of 150 mm. Determine the approximate smallest diameter of the beam and the power density at the focal point of the lens. The unfocused beam diameter is 50 mm.

(Electroheat Tutorials)

Solution

A helpful background is given in reference 64. Gas lasers exhibit weaker line-broadening mechanisms than solids, permitting broadening of the energy levels by only a few gigahertz. The low pressures used in gas lasers do not favour ion collision — induced broadening. Thus optical pumping, particularly of the type used with solid lasers cannot in general be used. Pumping of gas lasers is by electrical means by the controlled passage of pulsed or direct current through the gas.

The numerical part of the questions requires a statement of assumptions. The focusing of a laser beam is equivalent to the determination of the limit of resolution of a telescope and to a first approximation:

$$d = \frac{1.22\lambda.f}{D}$$

where D is the unfocused beam diameter and f the focal length (see, for example, chapter 14 reference 67) and the required beam smallest diameter is d.

However, with a more general analysis one obtains

$$d \fallingdotseq \frac{2.f.\lambda}{D}$$

(see reference 65, chapter 8, p. 317)

thus
$$d \fallingdotseq \frac{2 \times 150 \times 10.6 \times 10^{-6}}{50}$$

$$\fallingdotseq 63.6 \times 10^{-6} \, \text{m}$$

and the focused spot will be the smallest diameter.

The power density P at the focal point is given by:

$$P = \frac{10 \times 10^3}{\pi(63.6 \times 10^{-6})^2 .4}$$

$$\fallingdotseq 2.0 \times 10^8 \, \text{kW/m}^2$$

L2

Describe the difference between pulsed and continuous wave modes applied to lasers. What relationship would you expect to occur between the continuous output of a Nd: YAG laser and the input to its excitation Kr lamp?

Review the range over which lasers are currently available having regard to their principal wave outlets and power outputs. Describe the different industrial process requirements (kW/m^2) which can be met by lasers. Take any one such process and explain how a laser might be specified.

A neodymium laser operates at $1.06\,\mu m$. Describe how you would use this laser to produce a beam at $0.53\,\mu m$.

Solution
This question has a number of facets to which the student should be exposed. The excitation modes are covered in the basic texts (62, 63). The linear relationship between illumination source and laser output is discussed by Svelto (64) and Koechner (68).

A review of lasers can be prompted by the comparative table given by Harry (63).

The range of industrial processes possessing power density requirements in the range $10^7\,kW/m^2$ to $10^{10}\,kW/m^2$ involve cutting welding drilling and surface treatments of metals. Providing that sufficient power can be absorbed by the workpiece in the visible region of light then the laser can be used. Neodymium and CO_2 gas are two lasers frequently used in metallurgical applications.

The specification of the laser must have regard to its power and emissial wavelength outputs, the absorption properties of the workpiece and the rate at which the material is to be processed. The ability to achieve sharp focusing of the laser beam is an obvious requirement. The cutting of non-metals using gas jet, laser beam systems is discussed by Harry and Lunau (69) and is relevant to the question.

A very interesting background to the final part of the question involving frequency doubling is given by Beesley (70). He points out that as a beam of light propagates through a solid material electronic dipoles are formed within the atoms of the material. The strength of the dipoles, expressed as dipole moment per unit volume is given by:

$$P = \chi_1 E + \chi_2 E^2 + \chi_3 E^3 + \dots.$$

where χ is the 'polarisability'.

For the laser the oscillating field is of the form $E = \hat{E}.\sin \omega t$ and thus

$$P = \chi_1 \hat{E} \sin \omega t + \tfrac{1}{2}\chi_2 \hat{E}_0^2 (1 - \cos 2\omega t) + \ldots$$

and the second term can act as the source of second harmonics. The use of birefringent crystals and in particular barium strontium niobate permits selective destructive interference at the input frequency and the transmission of doubled frequency light.

L3

Suggest a method using two lasers whereby small movements of a surface on which can be supported a suitable mirror can be detected and measured.

Derive a simple expression covering this measurement perhaps suggesting some limits of the methods.

(*Reference 70 — modified by the author*)

Solution
Consider two surfaces X and Y. X will be defined as the reference surface and Y the surface whose movements relative to X we wish to detect.

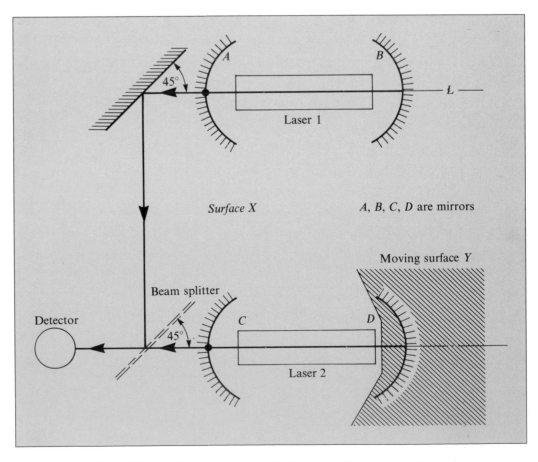

Figure L3. *Dual laser system for detection of small movements of a surface*

Figure L3 shows the suggested arrangement. Two lasers, 1 and 2 are allowed to produce outputs in such a way that interference between these outputs can be detected by a photomultiplier detector, which in turn receives the dual output through a beam splitter. All the equipment rests on the reference surface X with the exception of mirror D which is constrained to rest on surface Y.

Laser 1 is defined as the reference and a change in beat frequency between the two lasers will be detected as the surface Y moves.

If λ is the wavelength of laser light output in both cases and its frequency f.

L is the length of each (gas) cavity

C is the speed of light (3×10^8 m/s)

n is the number of wavelengths in each cavity.

then

$$\frac{n.\lambda}{2} = L$$

$$= \left[\frac{n.C}{f^2}\right]$$

from which

$$\left|\frac{dL}{df}\right| = \frac{nc}{f^2}$$

and

$$df = \frac{f}{L}.dL$$

Beat frequencies down to the audio range can be readily detected but in practice drift effects particularly in laser 1 (which would be stabilised) and more general thermal and microphonic effects would set a limit.

Supposing He−Ne lasers were used with a principal output wavelength of $0.632\,\mu$m their frequency would be

$$f = \frac{3 \times 10^8}{0.632 \times 10^{-6}} \text{ or } 474.\text{THz}$$

If the reference laser could be held within ± 2 MHz per day a measured 100 MHz beat frequency is detectable to a nominal 2% accuracy (and if the corresponding drift of laser 2 is additive, 4%).

These circumstances permit a movement of mirror D/surface Y to be given as

$$dL = \frac{df \times L}{L} = \frac{100 \times 10^6 \times 0.1}{4.74 \times 10^{14}}$$

$$\doteqdot 2 \times 10^{-8}\,\text{m for a 10 cm laser tube/cavity.}$$

The stability of a laser beam within the optical span of two concave mirrors, radii R_1, R_2, and separation distance L is given by:

$$0 \leqslant \left(1 - \frac{L}{R_1}\right)\left(1 - \frac{L}{R_2}\right) \leqslant 1$$

Describe what is meant by 'stability'.

The radius of curvature at Z along a Gaussian beam is given as:

$$R = Z + \frac{Z_0^2}{Z}$$

where Z_0 is a function of the optical system, and its width at Z as

$$w = \left[\frac{Z_0 \cdot \lambda}{\pi}\right]^{1/2} \cdot \left[1 + \left(\frac{Z}{Z_0}\right)^2\right]^{1/2}$$

Describe what you would expect to find within the above system, with a gas laser at the centre, perhaps by referring to the Rayleigh length.

An ionised-argon gas laser $[\lambda = 0.488 \, \mu\text{m}]$ has a mirror separation of 1.2 m and its spot or waist position is 0.6 m from one mirror whose radius of curvature is 2.0 m. Assume a Gaussian beam, find the radius of curvature of the second mirror. Is the system optically stable? Find the size of the beam at the exit point of the system on the second mirror and estimate the divergence angle as the beam leaves this point.

State how you might use this laser system in comparison with a carbon dioxide laser.

(*Electroheat Tutorials — the author*)

Solution

A ray generated within the laser system will oscillate between the two mirrors. Stability is defined as occurring so that when the ray 'oscillates' about the neutral axis it remains within a definable maximum excursion. Instability in this context leads to loss of light and extends the threshold conditions for laser operation.

A collumnated (laser) beam (Figure L4/1) will be constrained to a laser spot size w_0 and then widens. When the beam width area is twice that of the spot $(w = \sqrt{2}w_0)$ then the distance $2Z$ is known as the Rayleigh length and this length is a measure of how suitable the beam may be for various applications, eg communication signals.

For mirror (R_1) then

$$R_1 = 2.0 = 0.6 + \frac{Z_0^2}{0.6}$$

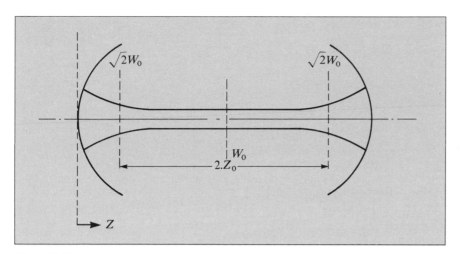

Figure L4/1

and

$$Z_0 = 0.9165$$

Giving

$$R_2 = 0.6 + \frac{(0.9165)^2}{0.6}$$

$$= 2.0 (= R_1).$$

Now stability is defined by

$$0 \leqslant \left(1 - \frac{1.2}{2}\right)^2 \leqslant 1$$

and the system is stable.

The width of the beam at the exit is:

$$W_e = \left(\frac{0.9165 \times 0.488 \times 10^{-6}}{\pi}\right) \cdot \left[1 + \left(\frac{0.6}{0.9165}\right)^2\right]^{1/2}$$

$$= 4.51 \times 10^{-4} \, \text{m}$$

The angle of divergence θ at Z is given by:

$$\theta = \frac{dw}{dz} = \left(\frac{Z_0 . \lambda}{\pi}\right)^{1/2} \cdot \frac{1}{2} \cdot \left[1 + \left(\frac{Z}{Z_0}\right)^2\right]^{-1/2} . 2Z$$

and

$$\theta = \left(\frac{0.9165 \times 0.488 \times 10^{-6}}{\pi}\right)^{1/2} \cdot \left(1 + \left(\frac{0.6}{0.9165}\right)^2\right)^{-1/2} . 0.6$$

$$= 1.89 \times 10^{-4} \, \text{radians}$$

The carbon dioxide laser has a CW output of $3-10^4$ watts and may be used for cutting and welding applications. The ionised argon gas laser with a lower CW output of 20 W would find application in ophthalmology and holography.

Background reading for this example is found in Chapter 8 of Siegman (65).

CHAPTER 9

Plasmas

9.1 Background to the teaching

Although plasmas have been the subject of much academic activity their application in industry is still in their infancy. Inevitably most books on plasmas deal with the physics of the phenomenon. Indeed the subject has grown so that there are even published series[71]. In such series the engineer will be drawn to books on fundamentals[72]. An alternative approach is to seek an introductory treatment in related books and in this connexion for high frequency plasmas Baden–Fuller is helpful[47] together with Ferraro and Plumpton[73]. Applications of plasmas are reasonably covered beginning with an early review by Gros B *et al.*[74] with more recently Ouellette *et al.*[75] and Ettlinger *et al.*[76]. An excellent review of plasmas for processing was made in 1983[77]. In 1971 Jordan[78] predicted correctly that induction plasma torches would receive much academic attention but their commercial future would be more uncertain. Nevertheless there are many areas where the plasma may play an important role and the principles should be taught so that acquired awareness will itself lead to application.

The air dc or low frequency ac plasma may be treated as a load with a negative voltage-current characteristic and its matching to a power source with a drooping characteristic provides a good example of how such situations can lead to instability (reference 6 lesson 11).

At the engineering undergraduate level the subject will probably be introduced in a descriptive way and the application references[74,75,76,77] should provide a reasonable source.

9.2 List of Worked Examples

PL.1. What is a plasma?

Define the term plasma frequency in the relationship:

$$f_p = \frac{1}{2\pi} \cdot \sqrt{\frac{n.e^2}{m.\varepsilon_0}}$$

where f_p = plasma frequency

n = population of electrons in a unit volume (say metre^3).

e = electron charge $[= 1.602 \times 10^{-19}C]$

m = electron mass $[= 9.109 \times 10^{-31}kg]$

ε_0 = permittivity constant $[= 8.8542 \times 10^{-12}F/m]$

Using elementary field theory or otherwise prove this relationship.

Calculate the plasma frequency of a discharge medium (gas) having an electron density of $6.1 \times 10^{11} m^{-3}$ and inductively coupled at 27.12 MHz. Assuming the discharge medium has a conductivity of 1800 S/m find the penetration depth (you may take $\mu_r = 1$).

How would you use this information to define the volume of a discharge suitable for a small industrial process?

(Electroheat Tutorials)

Solution

A plasma is a gaseous medium consisting of charged particles, light mobile electrons and comparatively stationary heavy ions. When the plasma is neutrally charged and without the presence of an external field there is a natural frequency of oscillation of the electrons. This frequency is termed plasma frequency.

A proof of the expression is given in reference 47. A simple proof takes the following form:

Consider a plasma of uniform electron and positive ion density. Let each electron be displaced a small distance s, within the boundaries of the plasma the electron density n remains constant. Relative to an axis (boundary) prior to the displacement there will now be a field caused by an excess of electrons after the displacement occurs so that on all electrons there is a restoring force eE where e is the electron charge.

Thus the equation of motion at this time of displacement is:

$$m\frac{\partial^2 s}{\partial t} = -e.E \qquad (1)$$

for an electron mass 'm'.

As the electrons are displaced there will be a perturbation in electron density δn and

$$\delta n \doteq n.\frac{\partial s}{\partial x}$$

In free space we have

$$\nabla^2 V = -\frac{\rho}{\varepsilon_0} \text{ where } \rho \text{ is the space charge density}$$

$$= -\frac{e.dn}{\varepsilon_0}$$

and in one dimensional space

$$\frac{\partial E}{\partial x} = \frac{en}{\varepsilon_0} \cdot \frac{\partial s}{\partial x} (\text{because } -\nabla V = E)$$

and

$$E = \frac{ens}{\varepsilon_0} \qquad (2)$$

so that combining 1 and 2

$$m\frac{\partial^2 s}{\partial t^2} = -\frac{e^2 ns}{\varepsilon_0}$$

and

$$f_p = \frac{1}{2\pi} \cdot \sqrt{\frac{ne^2}{m.\varepsilon_0}}$$

$$f_p = \frac{1}{2.\pi} \cdot \sqrt{\frac{6.1 \times 10^{11} \times 1.602^2 \times 10^{-3}}{9.109 \times 10^{-21} \times 8.8542 \times 10^{-12}}}$$

$$= 7\,\text{MHz}$$

The penetration depth defining the 'shell' of current flow is given by:

$$\delta = \sqrt{\frac{2}{\sigma.\omega.\mu_0.\mu_r}}$$

$$= \sqrt{\frac{2}{1800 \times 2\pi \times 27.12 \times 10^6 \times 4\pi \times 10^{-7}}}$$

$$= 2.27 \times 10^{-4}\ \text{metres}$$

This represents a very thin shell of conduction. The minimum diameter of such an rf plasma is at least 3.5 times the penetration depth (in this case about 1 mm!). Thus a containment tube of internal diameter of 30 mm or so can be used.

PL2

A dc arc/electrode combination is shown to have a characteristic of the form

$$V_{arc} = K_1 + K_2.l + \left[\frac{K_3 + K_4.l}{I_{arc}}\right]$$

where K_n are constants and V_{arc} and I_{arc} are the arc voltage and current and l is arc length.

The arc is fed from a power supply with a source resistance of 25 ohm and a maximum (open-circuit) voltage of 250 v.

Given the arc characteristic (Figure P2/1) CD discuss the maintenance of the arc discharge.

Graphically or otherwise determine the maximum source resistance of a 250 v supply to feed this arc system.

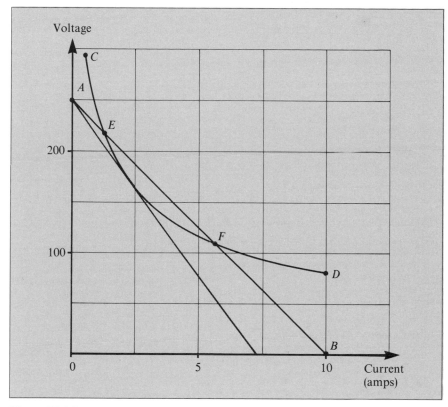

Figure PL2/1

Draw a simple diagram to link the constituent voltage drops along an arc length.

What is meant by the dynamic characteristic of an arc?

(The author)

Solution

The voltage-current characteristic of the power supply follows the line AB:

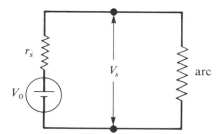

$$V_s = V_0 - 25.I$$

The arc and power supply characteristics intersect at points E and F where the arc and supply voltages are equal.

At point E if the current decreases there is insufficient supply voltage to maintain the arc, if the current increases the arc voltage decreases and the increasing difference between it and the supply voltage will drive the working point to the intersection point F. At point F any positive or negative increase in current will drive the working point of the arc back to F which becomes the point of stability.

By drawing the tangent to the curve CD which passes through A the current intercept is 7.3 amps. Thus the maximum source resistance to maintain the arc will be just less than:

$$R_{max} = \frac{250}{7.3} = 34.25 \text{ ohm}$$

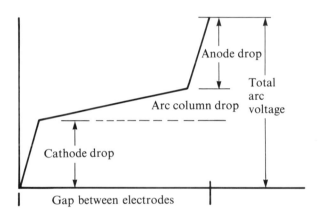

There are three basic areas of voltage drop, at the cathode and anode (with substantial drops) and along the arc column. Since the discharge exhibits good electrical conductivity it will possess a smaller drop than those at the electrodes.

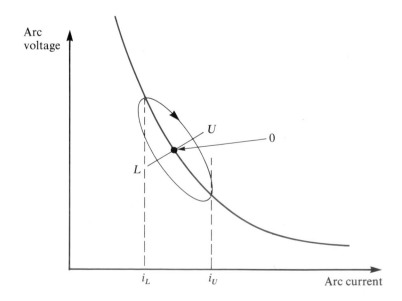

Taking a stable point of operation 0, any disturbance (air draught, minor electrical disturbance from the supply, electrode vibration) will cause sympathetic current changes. Even without these disturbances electrode temperature changes (mainly cathodic) causes a perturbation (providing arc extinction does not occur — see above theory for conditions of extinction) between currents i_u and i_L, usually elliptical in form. If the disturbance source is such as to increase this frequency of voltage-current relationship then $U - L$ is termed the dynamic characteristic. Since arc extinction will occur when the current passes through zero an alternating voltage supply will subject such an arc electrode combination to 100 arc extinctions per second and this in turn will lead to a non-linear current waveform introducing harmonics:

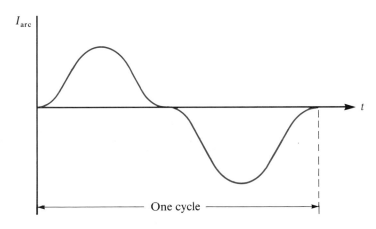

PL3

An empirical expression for the specific energy W_s to cut metal by a plasma jet is given by:

$$W_s = \frac{\pi.R.P}{2u.h.\rho}$$

where R = radius of jet

= half cut width

P = power density in incident jet

u = speed of cutting

h = thickness of metal

W_s = energy required per kilogram of metal removed

ρ = density of material

Deduce this expression and give some justification for it.

How would you specify a plasma cutting system to cut copper

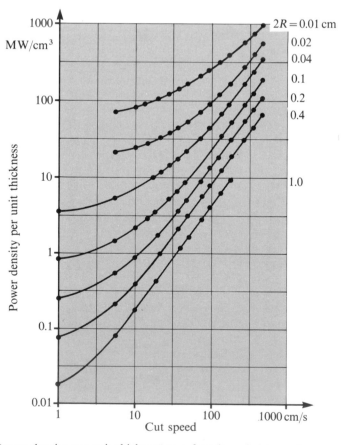

Power density per unit thickness as a function of cut speed, copper

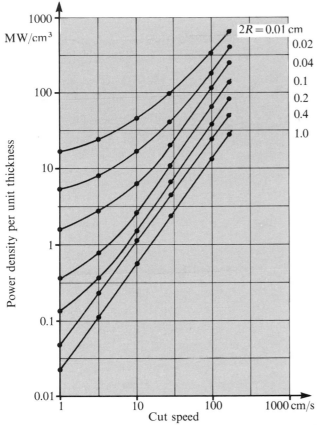

Power density per unit thickness as a function of cut speed, iron

sheet in the thickness range 1–2 cm at speeds up to 2 cm/s given ρ as 8933 kg/m^3 and a cut width of 1 mm.

How would your design compare qualitatively with a parallel system cutting iron or steel of the same thickness and at the same speeds?

Graphs of power density per unit thickness against cutting speed for both copper and iron are given.   (*The author*)

Solution

The approach recommended is that suggested by Bunting and Cornfield[79].

The plasma is regarded as a simple spot source of heat and therefore the power delivered is $\pi.R^2.P$.

The mass of metal removed per second is $u.h.2.R.\rho$

and
$$W_s = \frac{\pi.R.P}{2.u.h.\rho}$$

It is convenient to assume:

i)   The heat lost by radiation and other mechanisms is negligible.

ii)   The total power available in a focused spot is used to melt the removed volume.

iii) The power density is sufficient to meet the minimum total enthalpy of the instantaneous cut volume.

Using the given characteristic for $2R = 1$ mm and assuming 100% energy transfer (usually 70%) then the power density per cm (thickness) of copper is just over 1 MW/cm^3.

For 1 cm thick material the power required in the plasma jet will be

$$P = \frac{1 \times \pi R^2}{1}$$

$$= 1 \times \pi \times \frac{10^{-2}}{4}$$

$$= 7.85 \, \text{kW (say 11 kW for 70% efficiency)}$$

For 2 cm thick material *at the same cutting speed* the power required will be 22 kW. So a plasma rated at 22 kW is necessary.

The characteristics for iron give lower power densities (roughly 0.6 MW/cm^3 for $2R = 1$ mm) and so a lower rated plasma would suffice for cutting similar geometries in iron.

In general at low speeds materials with low thermal conductivities will lose less heat to the bulk of the material outside the cut region. At high speeds when such losses become negligible a high thermal conductivity will allow more heat to be conducted from the centre of the spot to the edge.

PL4

Compare the application of plasmas to two situations involving high energy transfer and low energy transfer, perhaps by reference to cutting and to gas cleaning.

How would you assess the specification of a power supply to feed a metal welding unit?

(*The author*)

Solution

The previous example and reference 70 may be quoted for the high energy transfer situation.

Precipitation of solids in gases depends on the attraction of particles to a charged body. Typically, plasma/corona phenomena occur as shown in Figure PL4.1 where V_i is the starting voltage to establish the corona.

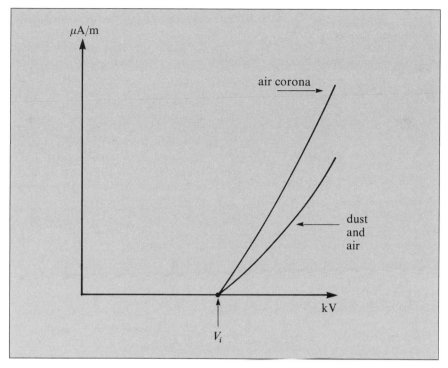

Figure PL4.1

A practical gas cleaning system will consist of a van de Graaf generator producing high voltages (8–10 MeV) using small currents to develop a corona which is sprayed onto an earthed moving conveyor belt or gas jet. This conveyor belt or gas jet transfers the charge to an electrode system which acts as the repository for the dust (reference 80).

Simpler systems use ionised wires fed by 12 kVdc with the wire matrix air purged into a filter collector system.

In the final part of the example its response will depend on the level of teaching.

The more elementary student would be expected to approach the answer by referring to a unit which delivers wire as the electrode to the work. By determining the enthalpy to achieve the molten state of the rod and by specifying the *rate* at which the rod must be melted a first (pessimistic) guide to power requirements can be made. There will be losses to be considered and additionally heat lost to the work (the area of weld of the work-piece will act as a heat sump) needs to be assessed.

More precisely, von Engel[80] treats the situation as the rod acting as the heat source into a semi-infinite solid medium.

Starting with the partial differential equation of thermal conduction in radial geometry for a rod he considers

$$\frac{\partial (rT)}{\partial t} = \alpha^2 \frac{\partial^2 (rT)}{\partial r^2} \quad \text{and} \quad \alpha^2 = \frac{k}{C}$$

α^2 is diffusivity in $m^2 s^{-1}$, k thermal conductivity $JK^{-1} m^{-1}$, C the specific heat per unit volume ('$C.\gamma$' of chapter 2) and r the spacial penetration of the heat into the work.

Von Engel continues this analysis by examining the droplet rate of formation and the mass/heat transfer into the work employing the solution to the conduction equation:

$$\frac{r}{r_0} \cdot \left[\frac{T_m - T_i}{T_0 - T_i}\right] = 1 - \left(\frac{2}{\pi}\right) \cdot \int_0^{u_m} \exp(-u^2) du$$

[$u = (1/2\alpha)(r - r_0)t^{1/2}$ and the integral is the error function]

This is quoted simply to show that the topic has been considered but its end use is dependent on empirical data namely the derivation of mean droplet mass rates expressed as a function of rod (welding) current.

Between these two extremes there lies the possibility of considering the heat flow down a uniform bar or rod again leading to the conduction equation (representing the welding rod)

$$\frac{\partial H}{\partial t} = \alpha^2 \frac{\partial^2 H}{\partial x^2}$$

H being a function of the temperature distribution at x and temperature t.

For a linear flow in a semi-infinite solid this gives the well-known skin effect equation for an input thermal function $h = H_0 \sin wt$ of

$$h(x, t) = H_0 \cdot \exp\left[-\sqrt{\frac{\omega_1}{2.h^2}} \cdot x\right] \cdot \sin\left[\omega.t - \sqrt{\frac{\omega}{2h^2}} \cdot x\right]$$

[for a proof see reference 43 p. 416 *et seq.*]

The semi-infinite solid represents the work-piece and H_0 at the surface must represent the heat required by the work at the point of weld to which must be added the (smaller) heat required by the welding rod.

Combining the two heating functions an assessment of power input can be made.

For an examination question some empirical data must be given perhaps using welding tables. For example for rod (wire) welding of mild steel 1.2 mm thick a wire 0.8 mm single pass with a dc arc of 19 volts 80 amp. is used. For 25 mm the wire increases to 1.6 mm, perhaps with a four pass routine and a maximum arc of 36 volts 420 amps. viz powers of 1.5 kW and 15 kW respectively. These powers can be assessed against the welding/thermal requirements of data provided for the wire (rod) and work-piece materials.

References

1. Carslaw H S, and Jaeger J C, *Conduction of Heat in Solids*. Oxford University Press, 1959.
2. Metaxas A C, and Meredith R J, *Industrial Microwave Heating*. Peter Peregrinus, London, 1983.
3. UIE, *Book of Worked Examples on Electroheat*. Kegel K (Editor), UIE, Paris 1983 (In German). English Translation. British National Committee of Electroheat, Millbank, London, 1985.
4. Edminister J A, *Electromagnetics*. Schaum Outline Series, McGraw-Hill, USA, 1979.
5. Buckley R V, *Electromagnetic Fields*. MacMillan, London, 1981.
6. 'Industrial Process Heating'. *IEE, Correspondence Course*. London, 1980 Edition.
7. Hobson L, *Electroheat References*. British National Committee of Electroheat. London, 1986.
8. External Publications 1970–1977. Supplement 1 1977–80; Supplement 2 1980–83. Electricity Council Research Centre, Capenhurst, near Chester CH1 6ES.
9. *Handbook of Electricity Supply Statistics*. Electricity Council, London (published annually).
10. Leach G, *et al. A low energy strategy for the UK*. International Institute for Environment and Development, 1979.
11. Davies C H, Submission to Sizewell 'B' Power Station Public Enquiry. Document P5 On Scenarios and Electricity Demand.
12. Barber H, and Harry J E, 'Electroheat: Electric Power for Industrial Process Heating'. *Proc. IEE* **126,** 11R, 1126–48, 1979.
13. 'Electricity Supply Handbook'. The Electrical Times, London, (published annually).
14. Hammond P, *Applied Magnetism*. Pergamon International Library, 1978.
15. Barber H, *Electroheat*. Granada Press, London, 1983.
16. Davies E J, *Direct Resistance Heating — A Teaching Monograph*. Electricity Council, London, 1987.
17. Horsely M E, Electricity Council Teaching Information Note 2. *The Electrode Boiler*, London, 1984.
18. Duckworth W E, and Hoyle G, *Electroslag refining*. Chapman and Hall, 1969.
19. Langman R D, Energy rate input control of arc furnaces. *JISI Vol. 204*, Dec. 1966, pp. 1194–99.
20 Davies E J, and Simpson P J, *Induction Heating Handbook*, McGraw-Hill, 1979.
21. Metaxas A C, 'A unified approach to the teaching of electro-magnetic heating of industrial materials'. *IJEEE Vol. 27*, pp. 101–118. Manchester UP, 1985.
22. Harry J E, Lesson 3 IEE Correspondence Course. *Industrial Process Heating and Electroheat*. (Part of Reference 6).
23. Horsley M E, Lesson 6 IEE Correspondence Course. *Industrial Process Heating and Electroheat*. (Part of Reference 6).
24. See for example Holman J P, *Heat Transfer*. McGraw Hill, 1981.
25. Hottel H C, Table A-23 from McAdams Heat Transmission 3rd Edition. McGraw Hill, 1954.
26. Barber H, Harry J E, and Hobson L, *Electric heating elements (unsheathed)*. Electricity Council Teaching Information Note 3 (1985).
27. Barber H, Harry J E, and Hobson L, *Electric heating elements (sheathed)*. Electricity Council Teaching Information Note 4 (1986).
28. Infra-red process heating (Guidelines for the manufacture and safe use of equipment in the presence of flammable vapours). British National Committee of Electroheat, London, 1985.
29. Safety guidelines for industrial electric immersion heaters. Application to heating liquids in open tanks and vats. British National Committee of Electroheat, London, 1985.
30. The application of electric infra-red heating to industrial processes. British National Committee of Electroheat, London, 1981.
31. Gray W A, and Müller R, *Engineering Calculations in Radiative Heat Transfer*. Pergamon Press, 1974.
32. Chantry, G W, *Long wave optics* (2 Volumes). Academic Press, 1984.
33. Hammack T J, and Jikuklinka S, 'Self-limiting electrical heat tracing: new solutions to old problems'. *IJEEE Trans. Ind. Appl.*, 1977, 1A–13 (2) March/April pp. 134–38.

34. Angel F, 'The technology of electric trace heating'. *Executive Engineer*, 1979, **61,** (3) pp. 15–17.
35. Hannington S T, 'Improved trace heaters for hazardous zones'. *Electr.* India 1983, **23,** (15) August pp. 27–30.
36. Tsappi P, and Langman R D, 'Resistance heating of steel tubes'. Montec 86.
37. Tsappi P, *Research Thesis — Aston University.*
38. Nicholls H J, *Induction Heating for introductory courses on electrical engineering.* Electricity Council Teaching Note No. 1.
39. Warren A G, *Mathematics applied to Electrical Engineering.* Chapman and Hall.
40. McLachlan N W, *Bessel Functions for Engineers.* Clarendon Press. Oxford, 1961.
41. Lozinskii M G, *Industrial applications of induction heating.* Pergamon, 1969.
42. Brown G H, Hoyler C N, and Bierwirth R A, *Theory and application of radio-frequency heating.* Van Nostrand 1947.
43. Pipes L A, and Harvill L R, *Applied Mathematics for Engineers and Physicists.* McGraw Hill 1970.
44. Davies E J, *Heat Transfer for Induction Heating.* Electricity Council Teaching Note No. 5.
45. Proceedings of a Tutorial Conference on Measurement of High Frequency Dielectric Properties of Materials. National Physical Laboratory, Teddington UK, March 1972, IPC Science and Technology Press Ltd.
46. Von Hippel A R, *Dielectric Materials and Applications*, John Wiley, New York, (1954).
47. Baden Fuller A J, *Microwaves.* Pergamon Press, London, 1979.
48. Ramo S, Whinnery J R, and van Duzer T, *Fields and Waves in Communication Electronics.* J. Wiley, 1965.
49. Paschkis V, and Persson J, *Industrial Electric Furnaces and Appliances.* Interscience Publishers, New York, 1960.
50. Burch C R, and Ryland-Davis N, *Theory of Eddy-Current Heating.* Ernest Benn, London, 1928.
51. Robiette A G E, *Electric Melting Practice.* Charles Griffin, London, 1972.
52. Duckworth W E, Steel Times Annual Review, 1968, 183.
53. Langman R D, and Wilford C F, *The channel furnace and its application in the iron foundry.* Journal Institute of British Foundrymen Silver Jubilee Edition 1979 (and the parallel Electricity Council Report ECRC. M1231 April 1979).
54. Langman R D, and Edgerley C J, *Progress in design of furnace power supply and control equipment.* BCIRA International Conference on Electric Melting and Holding Furnaces, Warwick 1980.
55. Moore D J, and Hunt J C R, *Turbulence and unsteadiness in the coreless induction furnace.* Institute of Metals Conference on metallurgical applications of magnetic hydrodynamics. Cambridge UK, September 1982.
56. Langman R D, *Papers on tonnage melting of metals.* International Conference of South African Institute of Mining and Metallurgy — Johannesburg June/July, 1975. (Available in UK as Electricity Council Research Centre Report M795 February 1975).
57. Swinden D J, *The Arc Furnace — A teaching monograph.* The Electricity Council (Third Edition, 1986).
58. Langman R D, *The supply of power to three-phase, electric-arc steelmaking furnaces.* South African Institute of Electrical Engineers, June, 1975.
59. Dixon G F L, and Kendall P G. 'Supply to arc furnaces: measurement and prediction of supply voltage fluctuation'. *Proc. IEE*, 1972, **119,** (4), April pp. 456–65.
60. *Supply to arc furnaces.* Engineering Recommendations P7/2. The Electricity Council.
61. Ravenscroft J, 'The determination of the electrical characteristics of an arc furnace' *Proc. IEE.*, 1961, **108,** Part A (38). April pp. 140–52.
62. Milne W I, *Lasers and their industrial application.* Electricity Council Teaching Monograph No. 2 4211/83.
63. Harry J E, *Industrial Lasers and their applications.* McGraw Hill, 1974.
64. Svelto O, and Hanna D C, (Editor). *Principles of Lasers.* Plenum Press, London, 1982.
65. Siegman A E, *An introduction to lasers and masers.* McGraw Hill, 1971.
66. Jenkins F A, and White H E, *Fundamentals of Optics.* McGraw Hill, 1981 Edition.
67. Longhurst R S, *Geometrical and physical optics.* Longmans, 1963.

68. Koechner W, 'Solid State Laser Engineering'. *Springer Series in Optical Engineering Vol. 1*, (Springer-Verlag, New York, Berlin, 1976).
69. Harry J E, and Lunau F W, 'Electrothermal cutting processes using a CO_2 laser'. *IEEE Trans.* Industry Applications 8(4), 418–24, 1972.
70. Beesley M J, *Lasers and their application.* Taylor and Francis, London, 1971.
71. See for example the Wiley series in plasma physics.
72. Nicholson D R, *Introduction to Plasma Theory.* John Wiley and Son, New York, 1983.
73. Ferraro V C A, and Plumpton C, *Magneto-fluid dynamics.* Oxford, 1966.
74. Gross B, Grycz B, and Miklossy K, *Plasma Technology.* Iliffe, London, 1968.
75. Ouellette R P, Barbier M M, and Cheremisinoff P N, *Electrotechnology, Volume 5.* 'Low Temperature Plasma Technology Applications'. Ann Arbor Science Publishers, Michigan, 1980.
76. Ettlinger L A, Nainan T D, Ouellette R P, and Cheremisinoff P N, *Electrotechnology, Volume 6.* 'High-Temperature Plasma Technology Applications'. Ann Arbor Science Publishers, Michigan 1980.
77. Szekely J, and Apelian D, (Editors), 'Plasma Processing and Synthesis of Materials'. *Materials Research Society, Symposia Proceedings, Volume 30.* North-Holland, New York, 1984.
78. Jordan G R, 'Induction plasma torches. *Rev. Phys. in Tech.*, 1971 **2**, (3) pp. 128–45.
79. Bunting K A, and Cornfield G, 'Toward a general theory of cutting: a relationship between the incident power density and the cut speed'. Paper 75-HT-W *Journal of Heat Transfer, ASME*, 1975.
80. von Engel A, *Electric Plasmas: Their nature and uses.* Taylor and Francis, London, 1983.

Reference has been made in the text to the Electricity Council Electroproduction Teaching Material involving Electroheat. The full list available in 1987 is:

Teaching Information Notes

Number	Title	Author(s)
TIN1	Induction Heating	Nicholls H J
TIN2	The Electrode Boiler	Horsley M E
TIN3	Electric heating elements (Unsheathed)	Barber H, Harry J E, and Hobson L
TIN4	Electric heating elements (Sheathed)	Barber H, Harry J E, and Hobson L
TIN5	Heat transfer for induction heating	Davies E J

Teaching Monographs

TM1	The arc furnace	Swinden D J
TM2	Lasers and their industrial applications	Milne W I
TM3	Direct Resistance Heating	Davies E J

Teaching Experiment Notes

TEN1	Radio-frequency Plastics Welding	Nicholls H J, Waggott R, and Langman R D
TEN2	Computer Control of a simple electro-thermal process	Langman R D

Additionally, the following documents issued by the
British National Committee for Electroheat

Electroheat References	Hobson L
The application of electric infra-red heating to industrial processes	Anon.
Infra-red process heating (Guidelines for the manufacture and safe use of equipment in the presence of flammable vapours)	Anon.
Safety Guidelines for industrial electric immersion heaters (application to heating liquids in open tanks and vats)	Anon.
Dielectric Heating for industrial processes.	Anon.